ROYAL AIR FORCE
GERMANY

Paul Jackson

LONDON
IAN ALLAN LTD

CONTENTS

First published 1986

ISBN 0 7110 1579 1

Published by Ian Allan Ltd, Shepperton, Surrey;
and printed by Ian Allan Printing Ltd at their works
at Coombelands in Runnymede, England

Front cover:
Harrier GR3. *Herman J. Sixma*

Front cover, inset:
The badge of RAF Germany.

Back cover, top to bottom:
Tornado GR1 ZD789 of No 17 Squadron.
Phantom FGR2 XV430 of No 19 Squadron.
Harrier GR3 XZ131 of No 4 Squadron.
Jaguar GR1 XZ101 of No 2 Squadron.
*These side views are reproduced by kind
permission of Squadron Prints. Copies of these
prints (size 11¼"×17½"), and many aircraft side
views are available from:* **Squadron Prints,
3 Torrington Avenue, Giffnock, Glasgow
G46 7LT.**

The illustrations for this book were supplied by RAF Germany
photographers Barry Elson and Geoff Card, Cpl Derek Booth
and Cpl Rick Brewell; Peter Gilchrist; the Andy Thomas
collection; and Paul Jackson.

INTRODUCTION

Despite the declining role of the United Kingdom in influencing world events, it may be claimed that at least some trappings remain of 'Global Power' status. One of these is the basing of armed forces outside the home country — in particular, on territory not of a former colony or protectorate. Part of the UK's sizeable 'up front' contribution to the security of Western Europe is in the German Federal Republic, where RAF Germany functions as an equal partner to the host country within the framework of NATO.

Mutual defence co-operation with a free Germany was an incomprehensible notion to the RAF personnel who established themselves on the aerodromes of a broken and defeated nation in the spring of 1945 — and when their HQ was named 'British Air Force of Occupation' there could be no doubting its function. However, as newly liberated Eastern Europe fell into the iron grip of another totalitarian regime and free Germany again embraced democracy, the role of resident British and Allied military components was transformed from occupiers into partners.

Today, RAF Germany is a vital element in the NATO front line and, operating from bases on the European mainland, tangible proof that Britain is fully committed to the defence of its friends and allies throughout the West. RAF Germany is equipped — as befits its role — with some of the Service's most advanced and potent combat equipment, and rehearsed to perfection in its operation. Without doubt it is the elite spearhead of a competent and respected fighting force.

Below:
NATO aircraft up to the size of a Transall C-160D have operated from strips of prepared autobahn during exercises, but none is more at home on such a surface than the Harrier.

1. BACKGROUND AND HISTORY

The nature of United Kingdom commitments to the defence of its allies in NATO is dependent in no small measure upon its geographical position. In any future European conflict — as in the last — the UK will serve as a base for strategic strike forces and reserves and as a collecting point for supplies and reinforcements. However, the psychological and practical aspects of deterrence demand that some elements be deployed 'up front' where they can reassure allies and potential enemies of Britain's resolve to resist aggression. Two such UK forces stand shoulder-to-shoulder with their NATO counterparts in Central Europe: the British Army of the Rhine (BAOR) and Royal Air Force Germany (RAFG).

Antecedents of both these commands arrived in Germany as conquerors; they remained as occupying forces and only later were transformed into allies. For the RAF, the story of its German component began in 1943 when the possibility was beginning to dawn of victory against Hitler's Third Reich.

Foreseeing the need for a fighter and light bomber force to pave the way for invasion of the European mainland and accompany its progress, in June 1943 the RAF formed the Tactical Air Force (TAF) within Fighter Command. Three Groups constituted the TAF, of which Nos 83 and 84 were already in Fighter Command, whilst No 2 Group was brought from Bomber Command to provide twin-engined attack potential. Autonomy of command came on 15 November 1943 when this force was renamed the Second Tactical Air Force and, after D-Day, its units operated from Continental airfields in proximity to allied ground forces.

The structure of the 2nd TAF was completed in August 1944 with the addition of No 85 Group for support, maintenance and administrative duties. From then until the surrender of May 1945, Spitfires, Mosquitos, Bostons, Typhoons and Mustangs of the 2nd TAF's four Groups flew innumerable close-support and tactical bombing sorties as the invaders thrust onwards into Germany. The 2nd TAF's headquarters arrived on German soil — at Süchteln — in April 1945, moving soon afterwards to Bad Eilsen. It was here that the transition to peace brought a change of title, when the British Air Force of Occupation (BAFO) was established on 15 July 1945.

BAFO began as an impressive force, its components including Australian, Belgian, French and Polish squadrons of

Above:
It was the Berlin Airlift which confirmed that RAFG's predecessor was more than merely an occupation force. Augmenting the Command, No 47 Squadron's Hastings C1s were based at Schleswigland between November 1948 and May 1949.

Below:
The end of an era. The SEPECAT Jaguar GR1 was withdrawn from strike/attack roles with RAF Germany in October 1985, having been replaced by Panavia Tornado GR1s. Only No 2 Squadron, nearest the camera, retains the type for tactical reconnaissance. The other four RAFG Jaguar units were (in ascending order) Nos 14, 17, 20 and 31 Squadrons.

Squadrons of RAF Germany

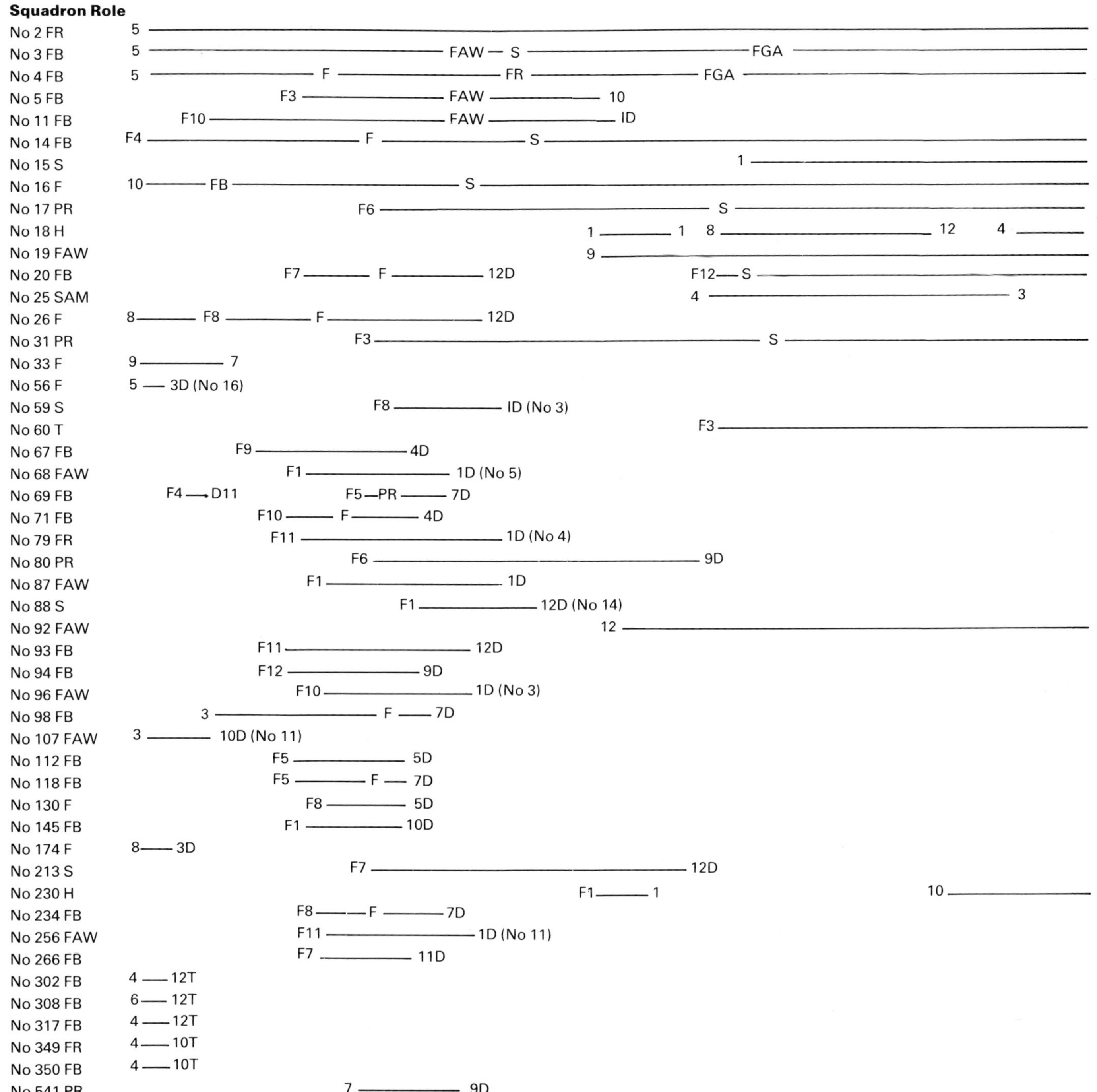

Squadrons of RAF Germany

Listed in the table are RAF squadrons resident in Germany with RAFG and its predecessors since 1945. The time attached to the Command is represented by a line, numbers at the beginning and end indicating the month. Units formed and/or disbanded in situ have the notation 'F' and 'D', whilst five foreign squadrons of the RAF were transferred (T) to their home air forces. Numbers quoted after a disbandment show units re-numbered within RAFG for historical reasons. As an example, No 59 Squadron formed in RAFG during August 1956 and was re-numbered as No 3 Squadron in January 1961.

Squadron roles on arrival in Germany are indicated after their number, and any subsequent change of tasking is shown at the appropriate time. Main roles are F=day fighter; FAW=all-weather fighter (including night fighter); FB=fighter-bomber; FGA=fighter, ground attack; FR=fighter reconnaissance; H=helicopter; PR=photo reconnaissance; S=strike/attack (including bomber-interdictor); and SAM=surface-to-air missile.

Squadrons not included in this table are those briefly based in Germany — particularly during 1945; units present for the Berlin Airlift; and Nos 102, 103, 104 and 149 which were in residence from 1954 to 1956 with Canberras, still under Bomber Command control.

Above left:
No 2 Squadron has a long tradition of providing tactical reconnaissance facilities to the RAF in Germany. Between 1950 and 1956 Gloster Meteor FR9s were operated in this role.

Above right:
Gütersloh, 1947: an RAF armoured car patrols lines of Nos 21 and 107 Squadron Mosquito FBVIs. Almost four decades later the RAF Regiment is again equipped with armoured vehicles and the Command's Tornado is a modern equivalent of the multi-role Mosquito.

Below:
Although it failed to live up to expectations as an interceptor fighter for UK defence, the Supermarine Swift served well in the tactical reconnaissance role with RAFG between 1956 and 1961. Swift FR5s were operated only by Nos 4 and 79 (illustrated) Squadrons at Jever and Gütersloh respectively.

the RAF as well as regular units. Rapidly, BAFO was run-down, from 34 first-line squadrons at the end of 1945 to 15 late in 1946 and just 10 a year later. Gradually the four Groups disbanded, leaving the Command in direct control of its depleted stock of squadrons. These retained their original tasking in addition to policing roles, and were five squadrons of light bomber Mosquitoes, four of day-fighter Tempests and one of Spitfires for reconnaissance.

The belligerent attitude of former Soviet allies in East Germany provoked an international crisis with the Soviet imposition of a blockade of Berlin during 1948-49. In the historic Airlift, which was the Western response, No 2 Group re-formed and BAFO squadrons were moved to forward bases in case of further escalation, but were not required. Reversal of the decline in strength was presaged by signature of the North Atlantic Treaty in April 1949, and within two years there were 16 squadrons in service — 13 of them with Vampires for fighter and ground-attack duties.

Further changes during 1951 included formal assignments of all combat aircraft to NATO's Supreme Allied Commander in Europe (SACEUR), but the greatest was in September of that year when BAFO returned to its former title of 2nd TAF. There was plenty of latitude for confusion in February 1952 as NATO's Allied Air Forces Central Europe (AAFCE) was sub-divided into the 2nd and 4th Allied Tactical Air Forces and 2nd TAF became part of the 2nd ATAF. Soon afterwards, No 83 Group re-formed to accommodate the build-up which, by the end of 1952, had reached 25 squadrons.

Quality as well as quantity was required to meet the demands of the Cold War. Having allowed fighter development to slip, Britain had to re-equip the 2nd TAF with Canadian-built North American F-86 Sabres to counter the MiGs deployed over the border until Hawker Hunters became available. In all, 13 squadrons received Hunters, two more had Supermarine Swifts for fighter-reconnaissance, and others took up the Gloster Javelin all-weather fighter to replace Gloster Meteors NF11s. The light bomber force re-equipped with Canberras, these being armed in the late-1950s with tactical nuclear weapons.

A rethink of the tactical situation had earlier drawn the conclusion that 2nd TAF bases were too close to the East German border and might be rapidly over-run with the initial momentum of an assault from the Eastern bloc. The solution was to construct new airfields as far as possible to the West, and these, Wildenrath, Brüggen, Geilenkirchen and Laarbruch, were commissioned between 1952 and 1955. Bases east of the Rhine were gradually given up — proving useful to the reborn Luftwaffe — and this process accelerated as 2nd TAF

strength was reduced from 500 to 224 aircraft in the wake of the infamous 1957 Defence White Paper.

The 2nd TAF headquarters too had been moved westwards, settling at its present location at Rheindahlen, near Mönchengladbach, on 4 October 1954. Eighteen squadrons — eight fighter, four interdictor and six reconnaissance — then constituted RAFG, yet by the end of 1962 only 12 were in being with just 142 aircraft on strength. An innovation during 1963 was the arrival of a squadron of Westland Whirlwind helicopters for army support, the task later being performed by Wessex. Two BAC Lightning squadrons were deployed in 1965 as the sole interceptors available to RAFG, and when they were concentrated on a single airfield in 1968, Geilenkirchen was handed over to the Luftwaffe. The base situation then assumed its present form: Brüggen, Laarbruch and Wildenrath west of the Rhine, and Gütersloh on the east side — plus, of course, Gatow in the British sector of Berlin functioning as an airhead with no based combat aircraft.

The first half of the 1970s was a hectic time for RAFG, involving the assimilation of four front-line types. All four nuclear-armed Canberra squadrons were replaced by McDonnell Douglas Phantoms from 1970 and Hawker Siddeley Buccaneers during the following year, whilst Harriers added

Above:
Long out-classed as a day fighter by MiG-15s based just over the border, the Gloster Meteor NF11 gave yeoman service in the night role until 1959. This, the personal aircraft of No 68 Squadron's CO, flew from Laarbruch with additional fin colours.

Below:
RAF Germany's first missile-armed interceptor was the Gloster Javelin FAW9, seen here in the markings of No 11 Squadron, based at Geilenkirchen. Main armament comprised four de Havilland Firestreak AAMs.

Bottom:
Nos 19 and 92 Squadrons flew their Lightning F2s to Germany in 1965 and operated the type until converted to Phantoms. No 92's colourful blue fins are seen here before the aircraft were converted to F2A standard and camouflaged olive drab.

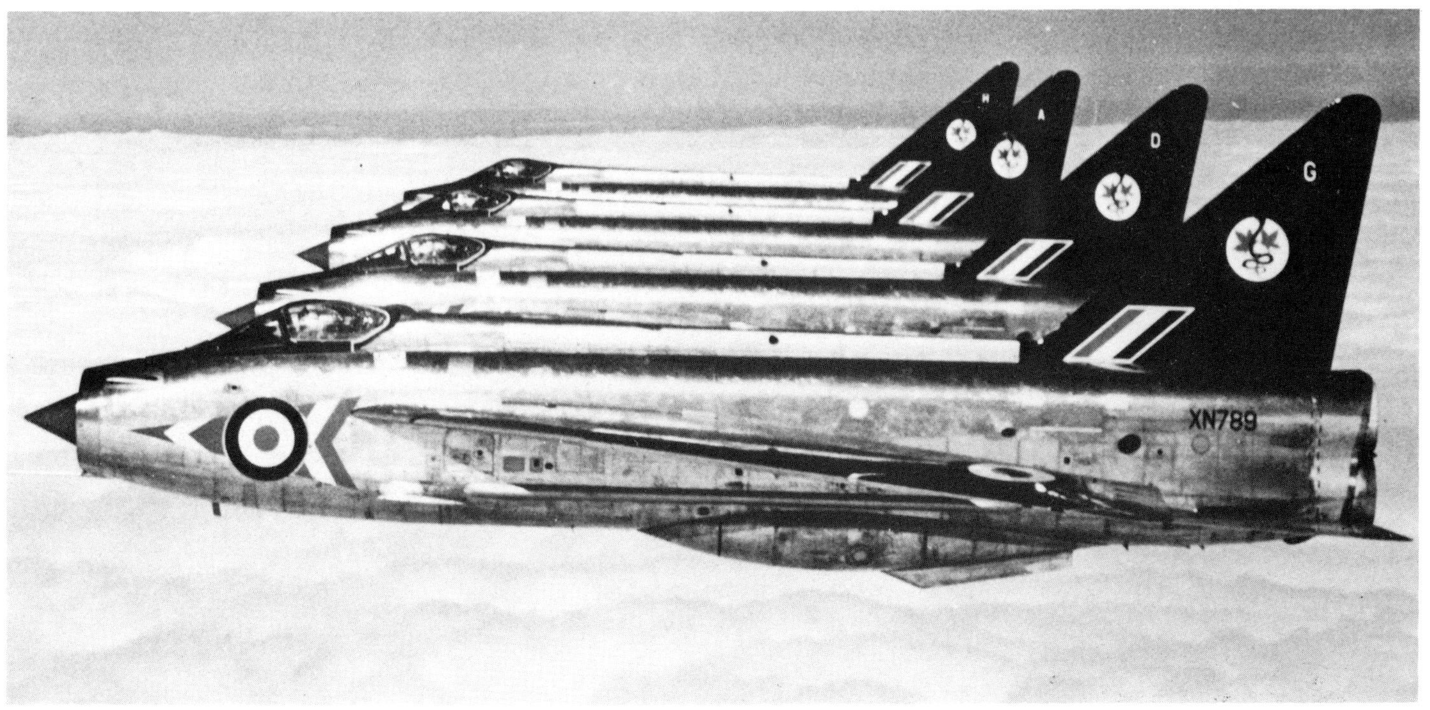

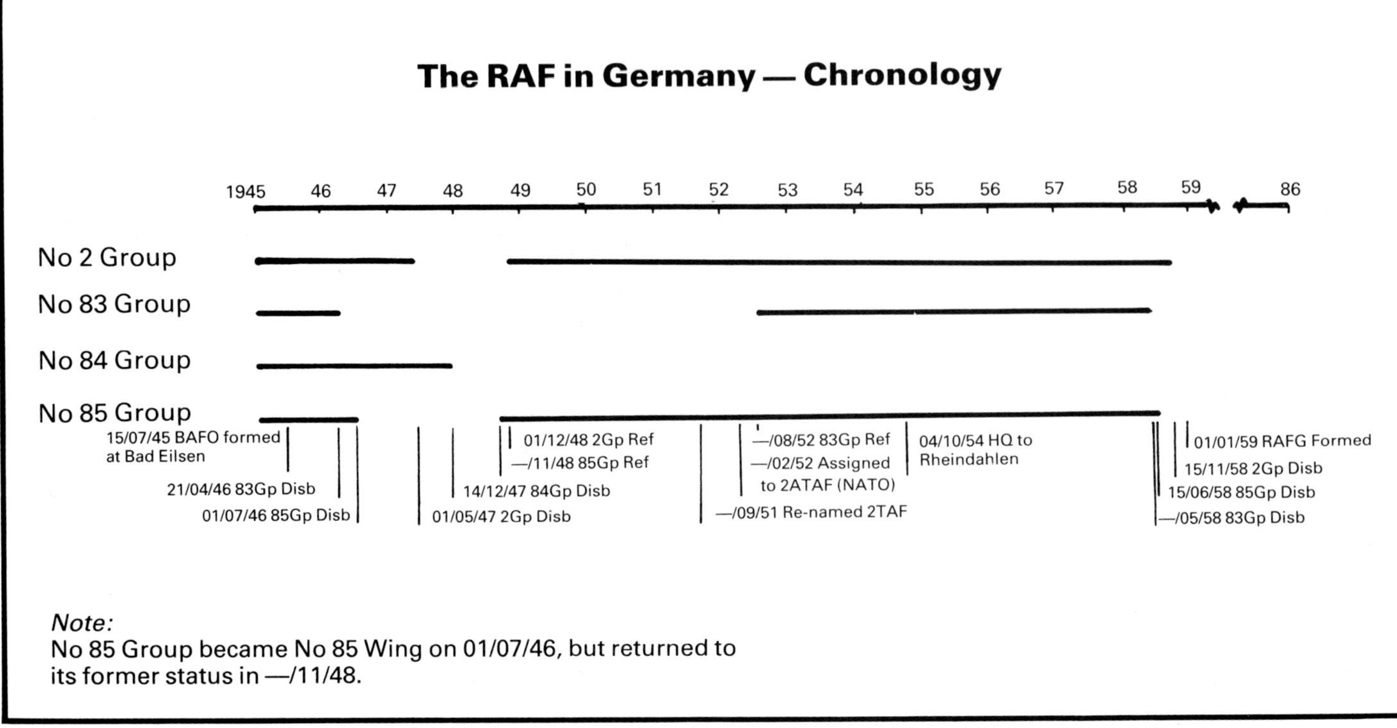

The RAF in Germany — Chronology

Note:
No 85 Group became No 85 Wing on 01/07/46, but returned to
its former status in —/11/48.

their unique STOVL potential, also in 1970. Phantoms were, however, a temporary issue pending availability of SEPECAT Jaguars, which began to replace them in 1975. A year later, in 1976, the Phantom was back — this time in the air defence role, replacing Lightnings.

In March 1977 the disposition of fixed-wing squadrons assumed its present appearance when one Harrier squadron converted to Jaguars and the remaining two vacated Wildenrath for Gütersloh. Operational strength then stood at two interceptor (Phantom), four strike/attack (Jaguar), two interdiction (Buccaneer), two close-support (Harrier) and one reconnaissance (Jaguar) squadrons. Not neglecting SAM defences, BAC Bloodhounds were added for base defence in 1971 and remained until the task was left entirely to the RAF Regiment's BAeD Rapiers in 1983.

Growing army requirements for airlift saw Wessex replaced by Pumas in 1980, these being supplemented by Chinooks during 1983 as an extra squadron was added to RAFG. Later that year, Panavia Tornados began arriving to replace Buccaneers and Jaguars, and form yet one more front-line unit. This process, though virtually complete, will not be finished until late 1987, by which time BAe Harrier GR5s will be replacing the earlier-generation version of the same aircraft. As always in over 40 years, RAFG is to receive the most modern equipment available to its parent Service, reflecting its role in the front line of Britain's — and Western Europe's — defence.

Below:
All-weather tactical nuclear strike potential was possessed by RAFG's fleet of Canberra B(I)8s during the 1960s. Although Phantoms, Jaguars and Tornados subsequently assumed the role, the No 3 Squadron aircraft shown was replaced by a Harrier.

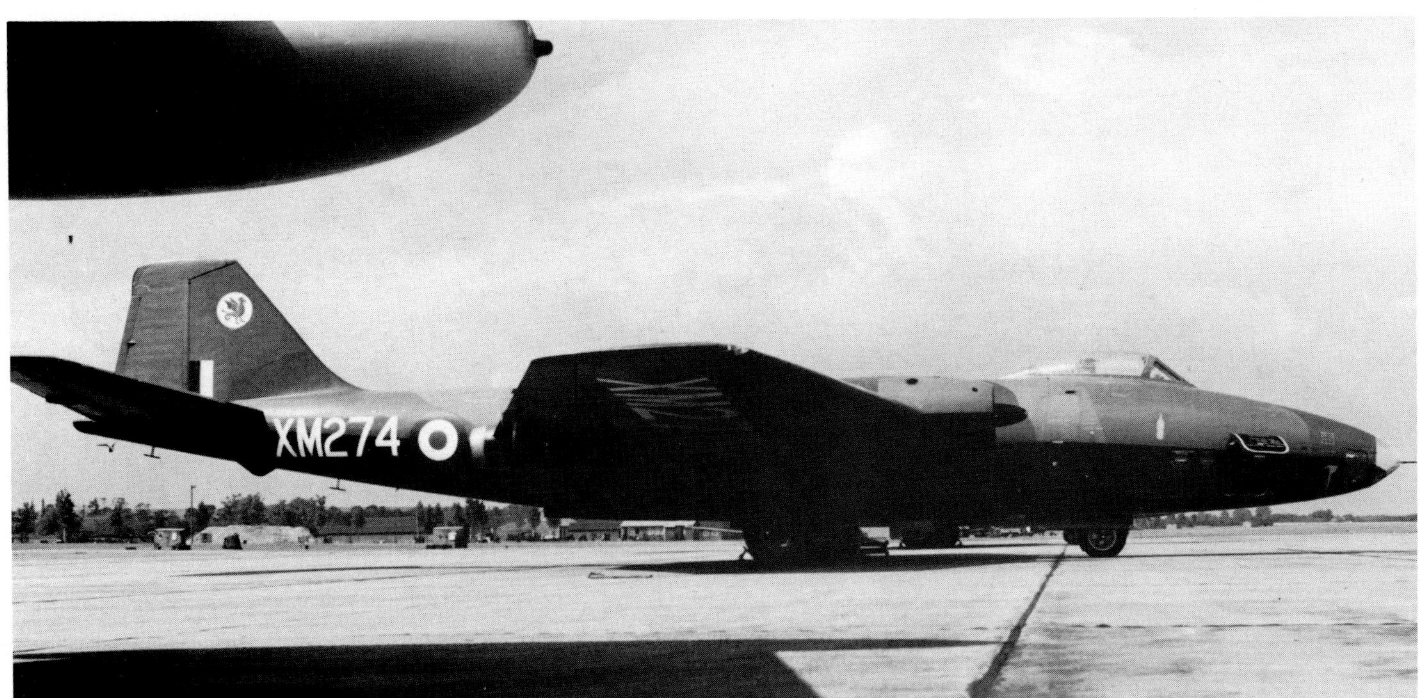

2. FUNCTION

For a nutshell description of RAF Germany's function it is necessary to search no farther than the motto included in the Command's badge: 'Keepers of the Peace'. The forebears of RAFG arrived in Germany at the very moment when peace was returning to Europe after six years of war, so a dedication to protecting the fruits of the Allies' sacrifices was most appropriate.

Though the aim of RAFG has remained unchanged through four decades, its outlook has undergone a profound transformation. During the first few years of BAFO, the RAF in Germany had resigned itself to becoming yet another of the half-forgotten policing forces in Britain's territories and possessions. Apart from the long task of clearing the debris of war and training the new personnel who were replacing those returning in droves to civilian life, a sense of purpose was lacking. Germany was broken and defeated, and the possibility of it threatening the peace of Europe again was remote in the extreme.

The consequent decline of combat strength was arrested, and a fresh impetus given to BAFO, when the Soviet Union initiated the blockade of Berlin in 1948. Since that time it has been the Soviet-dominated forces of Eastern Europe which have presented the threat to peace and constituted RAFG's raison d'etre. Occupation zones assigned to Britain, France and the United States have long since been merged into the Federal Republic of Germany, yet Britain still retains a national responsibility for protecting the air lanes into West Berlin, in parallel to the tasks it undertakes in close collaboration with its NATO allies.

RAFG's principal role is the provision of strike/attack, reconnaissance and air defence forces for allied air power and for the immediate support of any NATO operations — or, in peacetime, exercises — in the NATO Central Region as part of the Second Allied Tactical Air Force (TWOATAF). In addition, RAFG's two squadrons of helicopters are officially

Above:
No 15 Squadron was the first in RAFG to re-equip with the Tornado, and from the fin markings it can be seen that the unit prefers to be identified by the Roman numerals 'XV'. Dual control Tornado GR1(T) ZA446 'F' perpetuates squadron traditions in being named 'MacRobert's Reply' after a Short Stirling presented to No XV in 1941.

Below:
Following the re-equipment of two Buccaneer squadrons, RAFG began withdrawal of its Jaguars when No 20 Squadron converted to Tornado GR1s. In addition to carrying a pair of 330gal drop tanks, RAF Tornados are unique in having a further 120gal of capacity in the fin.

declared to NATO through TWOATAF, but normally placed in direct support of 1 (BR) Corps (ie, BAOR).

Fighter-interceptors, whilst providing an air cover force for NATO elements, have a national task to perform. It is a peculiar fact of life in both parts of Germany that Soviet rejection of the sovereignty given to the (Western) Federal Republic has resulted in expedients of 1945 being preserved in perpetuity. Thus (at the time of writing) Deputy Führer Rudolf Hess is guarded by troops of the four victorious nations

in an immense Berlin prison where he has for long been the sole inmate, and West German aircraft (civil as well as military) are prohibited from flying to Berlin.

Defence of three air corridors leading from Berlin to Hamburg, Hannover and Frankfurt is the responsibility of Britain, the US and France, although the last-mentioned no longer contributes to the task. The official form of words to describe this commitment is as follows:

'In peacetime, under the responsibilities retained by the United Kingdom pending the conclusion of a German peace treaty and in close integration with NATO, the defence of the integrity of the airspace of the Northern half of the Federal Republic of Germany and, with the United States Air Force and the French Air Force, the maintenance of access to Berlin in the three air corridors.'

Often overlooked is the vital RAFG role of providing an airhead for reinforcements — particularly during the transition-to-war (TTW) period of extreme tension just before hostilities are declared. Because of the ceiling placed on the number of personnel which can be lodged in West Germany (due to cost considerations), many of those required by RAFG and BAOR are based in Britain and must be brought speedily to their posts by sea and air. Three of RAFG's five aerodromes — Gatow (Berlin), Gütersloh and Wildenrath — are peacetime transport terminals whose traffic would be greatly increased during TTW by both military and charted civilian aircraft. Conveniently placed, Dusseldorf Airport would also act as an emergency reception point.

The threat to which RAFG and its NATO allies must respond is posed most immediately by the armed forces of German Democratic Republic (GDR) and the Group of Soviet Forces, Germany. The former has some 350 front-line aircraft for offensive and defensive operations, mostly MiG-21 'Fishbeds' and MiG-23 'Floggers', whereas the 16th Frontal Air Army attached to the GSFG has 1,200 modern aircraft and a high concentration of SAM defences. Efficient supply lines stretch through Poland to the Soviet Union, making reinforcement a far simpler task than would confront the US in attempting to move men and equipment across the Atlantic.

Potent all-weather strike aircraft such as the Su-24 'Fencer', supplemented by MiG-27 versions of the 'Flogger' and Su-17 'Fitters', are available to the Warsaw Pact forces for their first wartime priority of eliminating of NATO airfields, but equally worrying to the allies is the biological and chemical warfare threat, to which they have no direct parallel. NATO must, therefore, be prepared to fight at all times in uncomfortable and restricting protective clothing, whereas WarPac troops need only don such equipment immediately before their side uses these agents, and only in the region they plan to attack. The fact that whole WarPac divisions exercise in chemical warfare every year is of great concern to NATO. The threat is also changing, as evidenced by impending deliveries of Su-25 'Frogfoot' anti-armour aircraft and two new combat heli- copters (Mil-28 'Havoc' and Kamov 'Hokum') to complement the heavily-armed Mi-24 'Hind' in supporting WarPac armies.

Such is the initial momentum with which a short-notice WarPac attack may come, that NATO at first considered it impossible to beat back the invaders at the border. That 'fall-back' strategy of trading territory to gain time to re-group was partly responsible for the location of the 'Clutch' bases far to the west, but, of course, proved unpopular with the West German Government. The later 'trip wire' defensive plan called for early use of nuclear weapons to hold an advance nearer to the front. In 1968 that gave way to the 'flexible response' doctrine of conventional defence to a non-nuclear attack, and a similar effort to contain the enemy's advance and

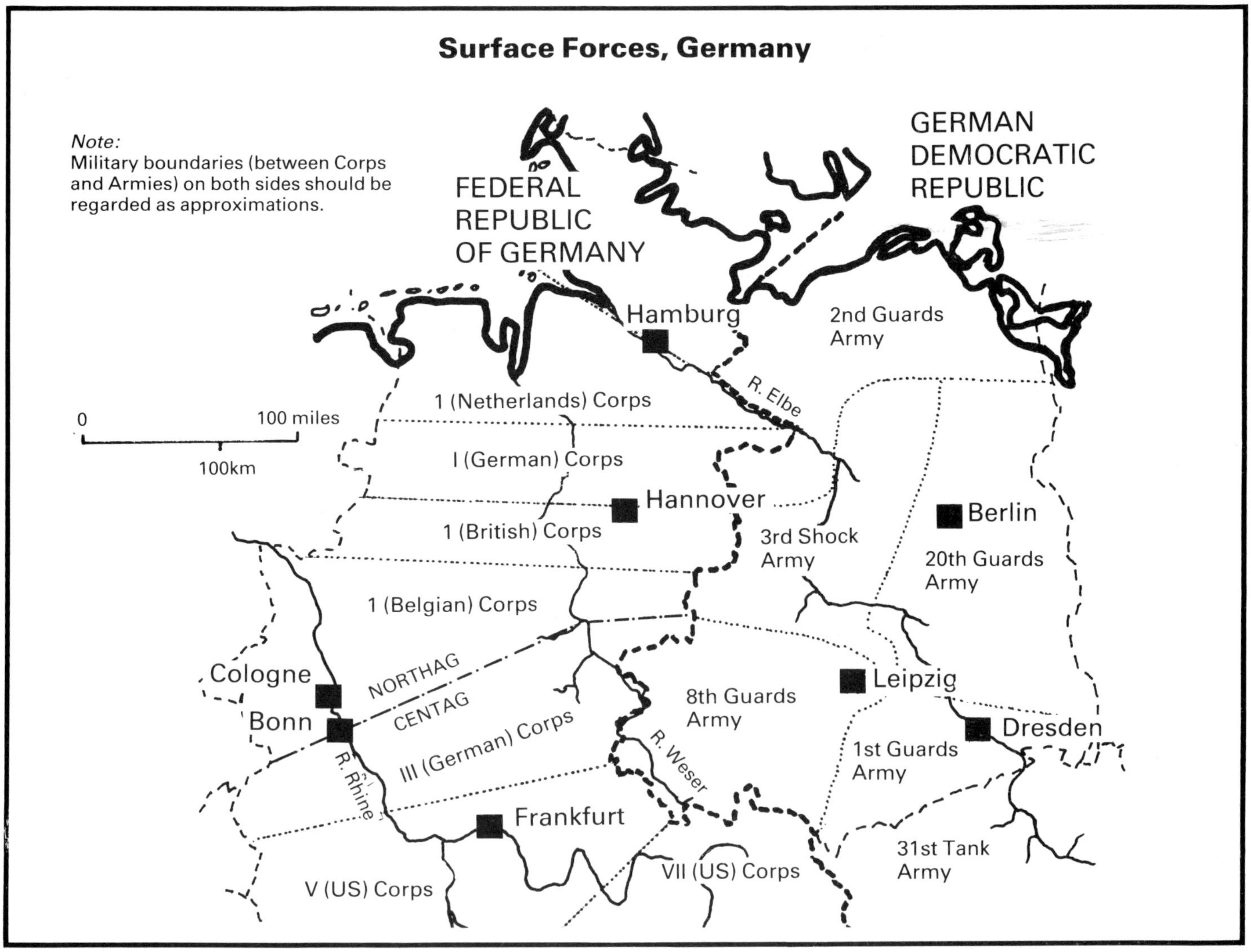

Surface Forces, Germany

so prevent most of West Germany from becoming a battlefield. Most recently, NATO has moved to FOFA (Follow-On Forces Attack), a strategy which requires the spearhead to be starved of reinforcements so that the invader cannot exploit his early gains. Now, the allies will not only attempt to prevent the battlefield from extending far into West

Below:
Battle Flight: No 19 Squadron's contribution to the two-aircraft team is pictured in its HAS close to the runway edge at Wildenrath. Unlike QRA Phantoms at home, it carries the SUU-23/A 20mm cannon pod as standard, in addition to the four under-wing AIM-9L Sidewinders and four belly-mounted Sky Flashes.

Above:
Harrier versatility is displayed to the full in deployments held three times per year. A short run is needed for take-off with maximum weapon load, but landing can be accomplished vertically.

Below:
No 4 Squadron personnel undertake routine servicing on Harriers outside their HAS. Three Harriers can be squeezed into a shelter, although there is then little room left to work on aircraft.

Germany, but they will also take the war into the aggressor's camp by interdiction (destroying his lines of communication) far to the rear.

The tactic could prove most effective against the Soviet form of attack, in which the spearhead force will fight until brought to a standstill, whereupon it is leapfrogged by fresh troops who exploit its gains before the defenders have time to re-group. Such a method of battle management relies upon meticulous timing, and so can be seriously hobbled by a carefully-formulated NATO policy of destroying key installations. FOFA demands tactical weaponry of extreme precision, so that a vehicle park or railway bridge perhaps hundreds of miles behind the front line can be destroyed in a single attack by a handful of aircraft. No lesser accuracy is needed for the counter-air role, in which the target is specifically an enemy airfield. Like the WarPac, NATO will mount counter-air operations at a very early stage in a conflict in a dual move to pre-empt a similar attack and prevent the opponent from establishing air superiority over the battlefield. It is therefore no exaggeration to say that stakes in the air war will be high during the opening stages of conflict.

The precision equipment required by NATO for FOFA and counter-air operations of pinpoint accuracy is now in the hands of RAFG in the form of the Panavia Tornado. The Tornado's role — which is, by implication, the major function of RAFG — is strike/attack against high-value targets. Both missions are identical in most respects, except that 'strike' involves delivery of nuclear weapons, whereas 'attack' uses conventional weaponry. Eventually eight of the RAF's 11 Tornado GR1 squadrons will be based in Germany, one having aircraft configured for additional reconnaissance duties.

Availability of the Tornado has greatly increased the flexibility of RAFG, particularly where all-weather operations are concerned. Hitherto, of seven strike/attack and reconnaissance squadrons, only two had radar-equipped, two-seat Buccaneers for accurate weapon delivery under all conditions. Jaguars, though fitted with an inertial navigation system presenting a moving map display to the single crew member, were insufficiently accurate for a long-range blind attack without external reference points en route. Low-level terrain-following capability is a further ace which the Tornado can play against WarPac defences, so boosting the chances of a

successful mission and increasing the aircraft's deterrent value. Having the advantage of two crew members to share the heavy workload when flying 'down amongst the weeds' in hostile airspace, the Tornado is well protected against interception through having jamming and chaff/flare decoy pods on outboard wing pylons, plus an AIM-9L Sidewinder AAM on each inboard pylon for self-defence. Attachment of all such aids to a Jaguar would leave it no room for its primary weaponry.

Close support is a second important role undertaken by RAFG and one in which it works hand-in-glove with the army. Whereas the effects of a strike/attack mission can take hours or days to have their effect on the front-line situation (slower arrival of reinforcements or less attacking aircraft), close support when properly undertaken is immediate — not to say spectacular. The two Harrier squadrons which are attached to RAFG have a well-known ability to operate away from regular airfields, giving them two clear advantages over more conventional aircraft. Firstly, the Harrier operating site is more difficult to find than an air base whose geographical co-ordinates are published in air navigation guides; and, secondly, the Harrier can be positioned close to the battle area to cut wasteful transit time and so maximise the sortie rate.

Equipped only with conventional weaponry, the Harrier responds to requests for fire support from the army. Contrary to popular belief, however, this does not involve the field commander picking up a telephone and asking a squadron leader for some Harriers. Even in wartime, requests have to pass along the combined NATO forces' chain of command so

Above:
Groundcrew of the Harrier Force must be able to effect an engine change in the field, as well as on base. The crane is required to remove the entire wing before the Pegasus Mk 103 can be lifted out.

Below:
Tactical reconnaissance is often a solitary duty which requires each pilot to exhibit a high degree of initiative. No 2 Squadron at Laarbruch is RAFG's principal recce unit, although one of the Harrier squadrons has a partial assignment.

that their priority can be assessed and duplication avoided. Nevertheless, once the aircraft have arrived on site they will often come under the control of a forward air controller (FAC) who will direct them to the point to be attacked — either by radio or by designating the target with a laser whose energy is picked-up by the Harrier's seeker. To ease inter-service co-operation, the FAC is often an attached RAF officer, whilst the Harrier flights all have their own army liaison officer.

Like the Tornados, Harriers may operate against choke points such as a river crossing being used by the enemy a few miles behind the front, or may be detailed to silence a gun battery which is pinning down allied troops. Examples of differing types of mission will be found in accounts of Harrier operations during the Falklands War, in which aircraft bombed fuel dumps and helicopter dispersal areas in the rear as well as attacking Argentine troops at Goose Green in very

A No 63 Squadron Rapier fire unit is readied for an airlift by a Chinook HC1 of No 18 Squadron.

Below:
The Puma's main task is light transport for 1 (BR) Corps, although it can also function in the SAR role with a winch mounted in the starboard doorway. Note the 'polyvalent' air intake filters now carried as standard.

close proximity to British soldiers. The latter mission, undertaken with great accuracy, demoralised the enemy as much as it raised the morale of the weary attackers, so contributing to victory in far greater measure than simply through the damage caused.

Air defence commitments are met by the two squadrons of McDonnell Douglas Phantom FGR2s based at Wildenrath. Having originally served RAFG in the strike/attack role until the Jaguar was ready for service, the versatile Phantom now performs air-to-air duties. With two crew members sharing the workload, and radar with a downwards-looking capability, it represents a considerable improvement over the Lightnings assigned to RAFG until 1976. Its armament comprises four short-range, heat-seeking Sidewinder AAMs; four medium-range, radar-guided Sky Flash AAMs; and a podded 20mm rotary cannon; thus endowing the aircraft with a broad variety of engagement options, day and night.

Perhaps the best-known function of RAFG's Phantoms is policing of the border area between the two Germanies. In view of the high level of tension between NATO and the WarPac, violations of airspace are regarded as a serious matter by both sides, and it is to avert a possibly serious incident that the Wildenrath squadrons maintain a Battle Flight. Technically correct, the 'Battle' description conveys an inaccurate impression, for the principal function of the Phantom is to keep Western aircraft in, not force Eastern intruders out. Singly or in combination, bad weather, failed navigation aids and inexperienced or 'weekend' pilots invariably result in local civilian aircraft occasionally heading for East Germany instead of their intended destination. Tasked with intercepting in the border zone any aircraft which does not have a flight plan or other form of express permission, the Phantoms are scrambled to intercept and shepherd the errant aviator back to safety.

Two airspace areas run parallel to the border, of which that farthest from East Germany is known as the Buffer Zone. Not having the irregularities of the land border, it is a reasonably straight strip, 30 nautical miles (34½ miles/55½km) wide, extending from Denmark in the north, past Czechoslovakia, and terminating at the Austrian border. Between the Buffer Zone and the geographical border is the Air Defence Identification Zone (ADIZ), the width of which varies considerably. (At Luneburg, near Hamburg, for example, it is 15 miles, but broadens to 70 miles a little farther south.) During their missions the Phantoms are kept under strict radar control and limited to not less than 10 nautical miles (11½ miles/18½km) from the border.

RAFG's air defence operation obviously differs from that in the UK, despite certain basic similarities. At Wildenrath the inter-squadron agreement is that each provides one aircraft for the Battle Flight on a 365 days-per-year basis. The duty pair are kept in purpose-built hangars close to the runway's edge, although the RAFG constructions are two of the standard hardened shelters, whereas in Britain some QRA (Quick Reaction Alert) hangars are less robust structures. Crews are allocated to the Battle Flight for a 24hr duty period, during the entirety of which they are almost fully kitted-up in order to be able to meet the five-minute readiness stipulation — the highest alert state in RAFG. UK-based counterparts usually have adequate warning from neighbouring allies of an impending penetration of their Air Defence Region and thus time to don flying equipment, make brief interception plans and walk to the aircraft. In RAFG the traditional 'scramble' from the nearby crew building is more normally the case, with mission planning undertaken in the air as the Phantom flies to the border, just 180 miles (290km) distant.

More often than not the alert proves to be a training exercise, for local civil aircraft usually generate only about two ADIZ violations per year. After intercepting the wayward aircraft, Phantoms fly a race-track pattern alongside (being

Right:
Rapier on watch. DN181 Blindfire radar gives the Rapier SAM an all-weather capability in the short-range air defence of RAFG bases. However, the two-man operating team remains a vital part of the weapon system.

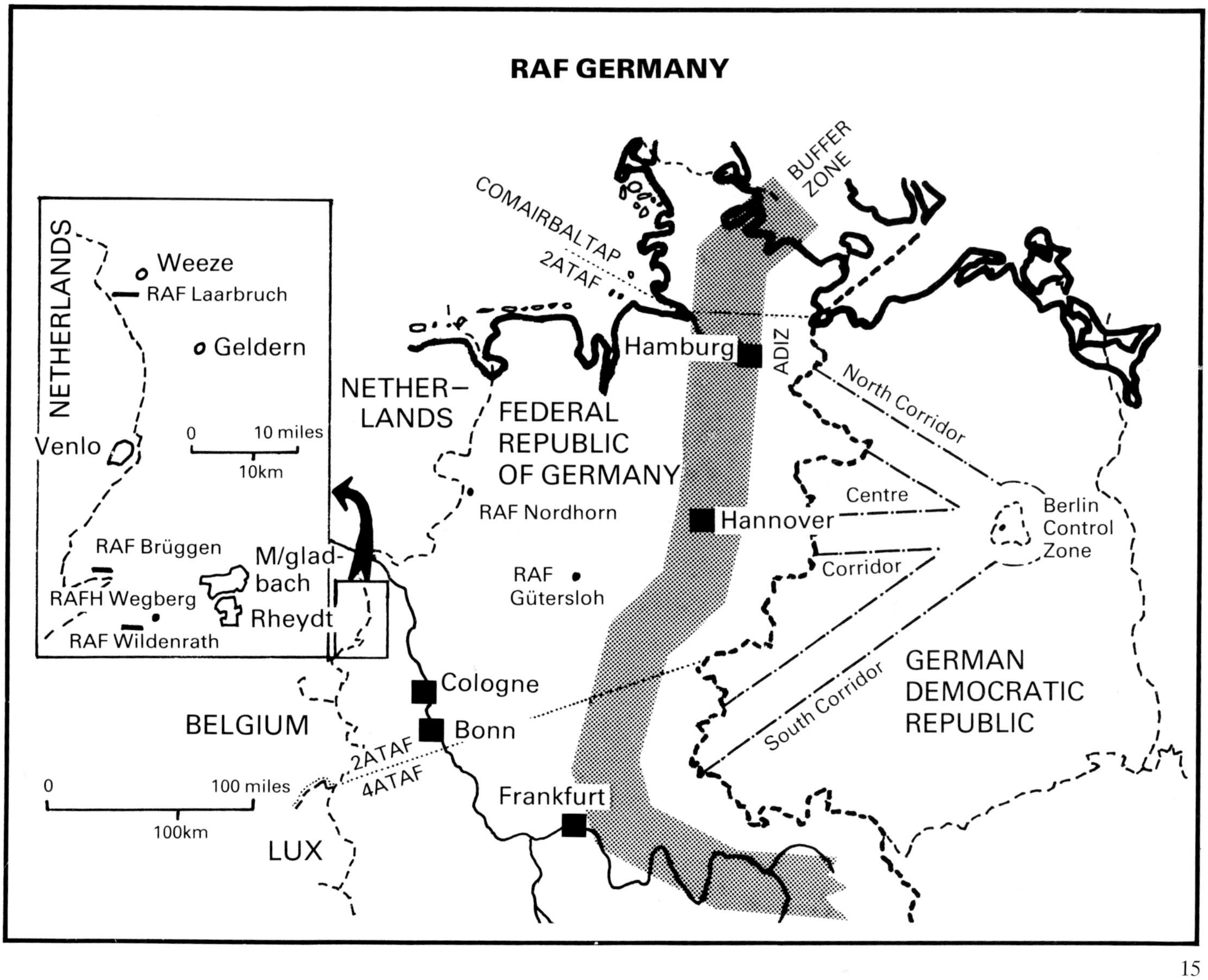

Above:
Ground security is the responsibility of the RAF Police, assisted in wartime by the RAF Regiment and armed personnel from the support branches. During exercises, duties have to be carried out wearing respirators, helmets and protective 'goon suits'.

somewhat faster than the average Cessna or Piper!) and guide it back to the West. The navigator will photograph the aircraft as evidence for the civilian court case which invariably follows, resulting in a stiff fine and/or loss of the pilot's licence. Phantom crews do not admit to having seen any Eastern bloc aircraft coming in the opposite direction, and presume that some form of equivalent force exists on the other side of the border. Most certainly, there is less civilian aviation in East Germany, and in view of the temptations to defect to the West it is unlikely that the interceptors on the other side of the border shoot only with cameras.

It would be distorting a mission description beyond the bounds of credulity to describe the de Havilland Chipmunk T10 as an 'air superiority aircraft', but this two-seat, piston-engined trainer certainly performs the task of 'air equality'. Two of these aircraft — the youngest of which was built in 1953 — are operated by the Station Flight at RAF Gatow, West Berlin, one of their main functions being to exercise Britain's right to fly in the Berlin Control Zone. Contrary to what may be supposed, the Zone does not cover just West Berlin but is described by a circle of 20-miles (32km) diameter centred on the Brandenburg Gate. Thus aircraft may fly over East Berlin and areas outside the city limits, subject only to the normal rules of air traffic safety.

Co-ordination of air movements is undertaken by the four-power (UK, US, French and Soviet) Berlin Air Safety Centre which, devoid of ideological bickering, is a fine example of East-West collaboration. As noted previously, Western air access to Berlin is by three corridors which are 20 miles (32km) wide — compared with the 10km (6 miles) width of civilian air lanes leaving Berlin in an easterly direction.

Whenever practicable, military aircraft visiting Berlin are persuaded to take a tour of the Control Zone to reinforce further their right to be there.

Chipmunks additionally perform a reconnaissance function as part of the intelligence-gathering process, but tactical reconnaissance for RAFG is undertaken by fast jet aircraft stationed at Laarbruch and Gütersloh. Forces are broadly divided into two levels or, more accurately, depths: Harriers taking the short-range missions as tasked by the commander of 1 (BR) Corps; and Jaguars flying longer distances. Of the two Harrier squadrons at Gütersloh, only No 4 has a 40% commitment to recce with a centreline camera pod, although all Harriers were built with a single fixed oblique camera. Harrier recce targets would most likely be in the immediate area of the battlefield and concern features of urgent importance to the land force commander.

This is not to say that the Jaguars go about their duties in a more leisurely manner, only that their missions are often flown against second-echelon forces in rear areas. These will not influence the land battle for a little while, but information on their whereabouts and movements will enable a timely attack to be mounted in the hope of ensuring that they never get to the front. Airfield recce is another Jaguar responsibility, as these installations are also in the rear for depth of protection, and such a mission might include SAM sites posing a threat to allied interdictor aircraft. As well as seeking targets, the Jaguar force is tasked with post-attack recce so that the results of an operation can be assessed. Returning to the scene of an attack can be a hazardous business, as any surviving defenders will be alert (and doubtless very angry!), but without this appraisal, NATO forces could be seriously misled if they considered each attack mission to have been 100% successful.

Post-attack recces are usually flown by a pair of aircraft, whilst the normal mission is conducted alone. This demands unusually high skills from the pilot, who must navigate accurately and record his own visual impressions of the target whilst eluding the defences without the protection of a wingman. Despite the sophistication of the Jaguar's camera pod (which, unlike the Harrier's, has IR linescan), the pilot's verbal report is of value during the subsequent interpretation phase. He must also have some knowledge of army equipment and tactics in order to derive maximum value from his time over enemy lines.

In spite of the high level of self-reliance expected from the recce pilot, certain basics of the mission will be dictated by higher authority. Tasking instructions to No 2 Squadron will include details of target position, category (one of 17 types) and the precise time to be overhead. Several pinpoint targets may be specified for one mission, in which case a reasonably safe route between them must be found. Alternatively, or as part of the mission, the pilot may be given a line search or an area search to conduct. In the former case, the Jaguar will photograph a single route (road or railway) to find out what is on the move; check the progress of a unit known to be travelling; or, in the case of a river, discover if a crossing is being attempted. An area search has the same function, with the obvious exception that the quarry could be within much wider boundaries. Obviously, the Jaguar will not conduct an area search in the manner of a peacetime photo-survey aircraft, but will fly an erratic course to confuse the defences.

In even closer contact with ground forces are the RAF's tactical helicopters: one squadron each of Pumas and Chinooks based at Gütersloh, yet ready to join the army in the field at a moment's notice. The Army Air Corps operates only light helicopters — Lynx for anti-tank roles, Gazelles for observation and liaison — and it is the RAF's responsibility to provide transport support. In peacetime some three-quarters of sorties flown are to collaborate with the army. No pretence is made to equal the German, US or French capability of airlifting a whole battalion at a time, and instead the helicopter force concentrates on assisting in specific, smaller areas.

During the TTW phase, helicopters would be engaged in distributing mines and explosives to sapper units and delivering certain key troops to their front-line bases. For this the several helicopters would be based at ports in the rear for collection of cargoes brought to the European mainland by sea. Wartime functions from forward bases include casualty evacuation; that vaguely-named task, 'special duties'; and rear area security. Recently, the Chinooks have been training with the rapid intervention forces of 6 Brigade and perfecting the methods of responding rapidly to attacks by Soviet commando-type units far behind the lines. The Chinook is also of value in being able to move a complete Rapier SAM fire unit in one sortie (crew and spare rounds included). It may, too, be conjectured that helicopters will be used as troop transports to exploit an enemy weakness — such as was the case in the Falklands War when one Chinook carried a gross overload of 81 men to secure a vital objective which the enemy had temporarily neglected to defend.

Assisting with security matters relevant to the air force is the RAF Regiment, whose duties encompass both air and ground defence. Protecting each airfield from air assault is a unit of Rapier SAMs — known as a SHORAD Squadron (Short Range Air Defence). Normally deployed to pre-selected sites just outside the airfield boundary, the Rapiers are assigned to the destruction of enemy aircraft which have evaded the forward lines of defence. Their targets are small, low and fast moving, so it is imperative that operators' aircraft recognition skills are to the highest standard: the proficiency test comprises 80 slides, friend and foe, and the mark required for a pass is not less than 100%.

Even so, elaborate measures are taken to ensure mistakes are not made, and it is because the Rapier is man-operated that standards are so high. A fully automatic system will shoot down friendly aircraft whose IFF is damaged or has not been switched on for some reason. Rapier operators follow up a negative IFF return with visual identification, and in the TTW stage might even withhold fire from a WarPac reconnaissance aircraft providing it is not seen to drop weapons. (Would that the Soviet Union adopt this restrained policy with civilian airliners at times of normal relations.) DN181 Blindfire radar gives capability at night when, of course, visual observation is limited. As an outpost, Rapier squadrons also perform the role of issuing the 'raid imminent' warning to their parent station and feeding observations into the NATO air defence picture.

On the ground, other Regiment squadrons are tasked with wartime defence of the airfield and its immediate surroundings or accompanying Harrier and helicopter detachments into the field. Light armoured squadrons are assigned to airfields and will patrol the area up to 3 miles (5km) away, using the guns of their Spartan armoured vehicles to project fire a similar distance again. Outside this 6-mile (10km) defensive area, allied armies and/or police forces are responsible for general security. More lightly armed Regiment personnel defend detachments and are responsible for advising station commanders on security. The latter involves placement of fences and barricades to protect key installations within the perimeter and training airmen and airwomen in the use of small arms. Everyone in RAFG except medical workers and chaplains is classified as combatant. If war should come, the pay clerk will put down his calculator, pick up a rifle and NBC suit, and take his turn in guarding the perimeter fence.

Below:
It is impossible to keep a HAS free of NBC contamination, so groundcrew and pilots must wear respirators even when protected from conventional bombs by a hard concrete and metal shell.

In both peace and war the welfare of RAFG is the prime function of RAF Hospital, Wegberg. Staffed by 300 Service personnel and 200 civilians, it has a normal complement of 230 beds, tends 7,000 in-patients per year and conducts 36,000 out-patient consultations in the same period. Wegberg is close to Wildenrath and responsible for all British Government employees at Rheindahlen and as far afield as the Embassy in Bonn. (The army takes similar care of personnel farther forward under a plan implemented in 1962, so Gütersloh comes under its area.) All required aspects of treatment (including some 1,000 births per year to dependents) except chest and brain surgery are available at Wegberg, but pupils of the attached School of Nursing have to return to the UK for geriatric experience before taking their SEN examination. The few patients requiring specialist attention in Britain, and those sent home to recuperate, are flown out from Wildenrath by a regular Andover service, although one of the local Pembrokes is available in an emergency. Wegberg also possesses one of RAFG's lesser known airfields — complete with wooden hut, name-board and windsleeve — this only being of grass and suitable for helicopters and light planes.

In TTW, Wegberg becomes No 1 War Hospital and adds a further 150 beds in its broad corridors. Reinforcements are brought out from Britain, 350 of them to form No 2 War Hospital. This has its equipment pre-located in Germany (at No 431 MU, Bruggen) and would be established in an army base near Gütersloh. Also to be deployed from the UK would be the 60 or so personnel of No 1 Aeromedical Evacuation Squadron, who are skilled in loading the injured aboard aircraft. Even the RAFG Band would leave its instruments at Rheindahlen and assist in para-medical aspects such as first aid and stretcher-carrying.

Two further units contribute to the functioning of RAFG in their own different ways. Bruggen-based No 431 Maintenance Unit stores, maintains and issues virtually the entire requirements of the Command from armament to furniture for married quarters. Its organisation will be described in the following chapter. No 60 Squadron, at Wildenrath, flies the RAF's last Hunting-Percival Pembrokes, primarily on VIP communications missions — one of the seven always being on hand for the C-in-C's personal use. Separate from other units in not being declared to NATO, it has secondary functions of passenger/light freighting and the occasional aeromedical evacuation. Squadron ground personnel are additionally tasked with servicing the numerous and very different types of NATO and civilian charter aircraft visiting their base and would undertake similar support during a conflict. Despite some hard thinking, the tacticians have yet to determine a wartime role for the venerable Pembroke.

This is the exception which proves the rule. RAFG is trained and drilled as a fighting machine and carries no passengers in the colloquial sense. Each unit, each man and woman, has a role to play in the maintenance of a credible deterrent force for Western Europe. Without doubt, the Command is the most finely honed edge of the RAF's 'sharp end'.

Above:
No 60 Squadron is RAFG's light transport unit, with main roles of VIP and communications flying. Three of its seven Pembroke C1s and C(PR)1s are here seen in their hangar at Wildenrath. A further responsibility of the squadron is turn-round servicing of the many and varied visitors to the station.

Below:
RAF Hospital Wegberg has almost all the departments of a modern civilian general hospital, plus a wartime commitment to the care of casualties. Additionally, it is involved in aviation medicine and has a chamber for regular checking of aircrew tolerances to decompression. Army Air Corps fliers also take advantage of the facility.

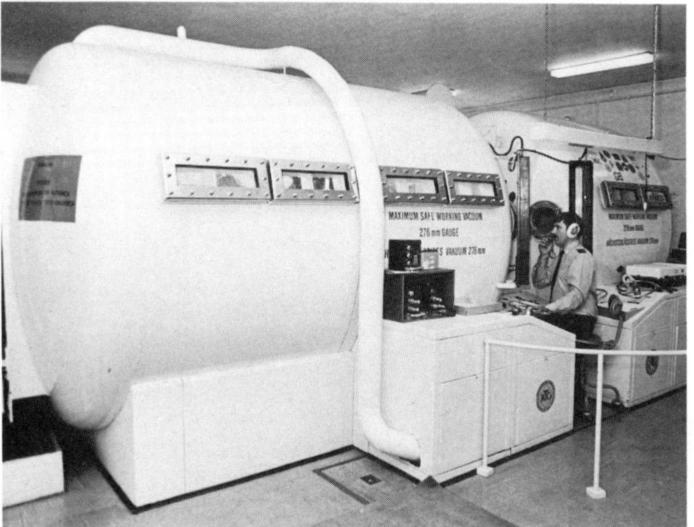

The 140 front-line aircraft and 11,500 uniformed personnel of RAFG function as part of two air forces — one national, one NATO. Simplifying (or confusing) the situation, their immediate commander is the same officer wearing different 'hats' to suit the occasion. To place the Command in perspective, it is therefore necessary to look at the organisation both of the RAF's and NATO's tactical air forces in Central Europe.

Within the national structure, RAFG occupies a position of equal status to the home-based Strike Command and Support Command as one of the RAF's three remaining major formations. Its Commander-in-Chief is an officer of Air Marshal rank, currently Sir David Parry-Evans KCB, CBE, RAF, who was appointed on 1 July 1985. Like several of his predecessors, Sir David was formerly responsible for one of Strike Command's component Groups, although his career began in the maritime reconnaissance world with Shackletons. Appointed CO of Victor-equipped No 214 Squadron in 1974, he was rapidly promoted to station commander at Marham, then to a series of MoD positions. Following a tour as Commandant of the Staff College at Bracknell, he became AOC of No 1 Group at Bawtry in December 1982, remaining in the same position after the Group HQ moved to Upavon and combined with No 38 Group in November 1983.

Routine matters within RAFG are delegated to the Deputy Commander, who is of Air Vice Marshal rank and therefore equivalent to the commanders of home-based Nos 1 and 11 Groups. (The third Strike Command component, No 18 Group, is adminstered by an Air Marshal who also holds a NATO appointment.) Below the HQ administrative level are the five aerodromes of RAFG, each responsible for its own based units (if any). Also controlled directly by HQ are the smaller RAF components: RAF Rheindahlen (the military township); RAF Nordhorn weapons range; RAF Hospital Wegberg; RAF Servicing Unit Decimomannu (the armament practice and air combat manoeuvring camp in Sardinia); and the RAF personnel attached to SHAPE, HQ AFCENT and HQ AAFCE.

NATO formations normally include elements from more than one country, and in Europe the controlling authority is Supreme Headquarters Allied Powers Europe (SHAPE) at Casteau, Belgium, which is the base of the Supreme Allied Commander Europe (SACEUR). Under SACEUR, NATO's armed forces are grouped into three regional commands (AFNORTH, AFCENT, AFSOUTH), each controlling land and air units. (RAF Strike Command is a non-standard direct-reporting attachment, known as UKAIR). Allied Air Forces Central Europe (AAFCE) at Ramstein, West Germany, is the flying branch of AFCENT and is divided for convenience into two geographical elements. These two are the 2nd Allied Tactical Air Force (TWOATAF) and 4th ATAF (FOURATAF), located at Mönchengladbach (or, more specifically, the Rheindhalen military township) and Ramstein, respectively. The allied ground forces are similarly split, so that TWOATAF works in conjunction with Northern Army Group (NORTHAG) in northern Germany; and FOURATAF with Central Army Group (CENTAG) in the south of Germany.

TWOATAF was formed in 1952 from the Belgian and Netherlands air forces, plus the RAF units in Germany. Two

Above:
Air Marshal Sir David Parry-Evans KCB, CBE, RAF was appointed to command RAFG in July 1985, replacing Sir Patrick Hine. The officer heading RAFG automatically assumes the NATO post of C-in-C TWOATAF.

Right:
The badge of RAF Germany.

RAF Germany Organisation

years later, it expanded with the addition of a USAF component, and gathered further strength in 1958 when some northern wings of the re-formed Federal German Luftwaffe were declared to NATO. Charged with conducting wartime defensive and offensive operations over northern Germany, Belgium and the Netherlands, TWOATAF is responsible for some 60,000sq miles (155,400sq km) of territory. This begins at the East German frontier, extends as far as the Danish border, covers part of the North Sea, runs along the Belgian border with France up to the northern tip of Luxembourg, then in a straight line northeast to the Iron Curtain near Göttingen.

Under the Alliance policy of shared command, TWOATAF is placed in the hands of the RAF officer who is C-in-C RAFG, so both formations have their peacetime HQs at Rheindahlen. Apart from air defence forces, which are permanently controlled by NATO, the components of TWOATAF remain under command of their various national governments until required.

At a predetermined point in the deterioration of relations between East and West, when war appears to be imminent, TWOATAF's combat HQ, the Joint Operations Centre, is activated at an undisclosed location just over the border in the Netherlands and the C-in-C RAFG takes charge of his forces there under the NATO title of COMTWOATAF. RAFG, which represents 35% of the RAF's front-line aircraft, provides 20% of TWOATAF's in-theatre forces. In addition, however, war reinforcements would be provided by the USAF and RAF. Rheindahlen continues to have a role after the C-in-C has taken up his NATO position, being then responsible for co-ordinating the supply of equipment for RAFG aerodromes.

The four principal flying bases have already received brief mention. They are Brüggen, Laarbruch and Wildenrath, all close to the Dutch border and collectively known as the 'Clutch' bases; and Gütersloh, east of the Rhine. Encapsulating the tactical situation in a sentence, RAF planners note that the 'Clutch' airfields are only 18 minutes from the East German border for a Sukhoi 'Fencer' interdictor — and Gütersloh only half that. Taken individually, the flying stations are:

Brüggen

One of the two strike/attack bases (with Laarbruch), Brüggen was carved out of forest and constructed on drained marshland in the remarkably short period of 12 months. Work started in July 1952 and the first RAF man moved into the station on 25 May 1953. It currently has a uniformed staff of 2,715, assisted by 340 German and 156 Dutch civilians, and is additionally responsible for 3,680 UK dependents. RAF personnel are normally posted to Germany for 2½-3 years, and the Command enjoys priority in the allocation of both men and supplies — escaping, for example, the worst of the fuel cuts imposed for 1984-85. Until recently, Brüggen had four Jaguar squadrons (the first of which, No 14, received its initial aircraft on 9 April 1975), but principal equipment is now the Tornado GR1.

The first Tornado arrived in June 1984 for No 31 Squadron, further aircraft going to Nos 17 and 14 Squadrons (in that order) before the end of 1985. A fourth Jaguar unit, No 20, held its disbandment parade on 29 June 1984 (becoming a Tornado squadron at Laarbruch on the same day), but was replaced in June 1986 by No 9. The latter was the RAF's initial

Above:
Brüggen's Tornado GR1 wing comprises Nos 14, 17 and 31 Squadrons. Markings of a winged plate, a gauntlet and a mullet (star) respectively appear on their aircraft.

operational Tornado GR1 unit and formed at Honington, Suffolk, in June 1982. The Tornado position is therefore:

Squadron	First aircraft/date	Re-formed
No 9	ZD809 'AA' Dec 85	1 Jun 82 (in UK)
No 14	ZD842 'BZ' 11 Apr 85	1 Nov 85
No 17	ZD742 'CY' 16 Aug 84	early 85
No 31	ZD712 'DZ' 13 Jun 84	1 Nov 84

Each squadron is equipped with 12 or 13 aircraft, including a pair of Tornado GR1(T) dual control versions for continuation training. Identification of squadrons may be made both from their insignia and the two-letter codes worn on the fin, these running from A to Z prefixed by a squadron identifier. Thus No 14 Squadron's aircraft are marked from BA to BZ, it being usual for the GR1(T)s to employ the last two letters of the alphabet. No 9 Squadron moved only its personnel to RAFG, taking over a fresh batch of Tornados on arrival. Also resident at Brüggen are No 431 Maintenance Unit and the Rapier SAMs of No 37 Squadron, RAF Regiment.

Above:
One of two Phantom FGR2 units operating out of
RAF Wildenrath is No 19 Squadron, a representative aircraft
of which is XV476/L, seen here on finals.   *Peter R. Foster*

Below:
A Tornado GR1 outside its Hardened Aircraft Shelter (HAS) at
RAF Brüggen. Marconi Skyshadow (port) and BOZ
chaff/flare (starboard) ECM pods are carried on the outboard
wing pylons.   *Herman J. Sixma (IAAP)*

Gatow

This has the singular distinction of being the only RAF station which had its opening ceremony performed by Adolf Hitler! Admittedly this was in 1935, when it was the Luftwaffe's main aircrew training centre. Captured by Soviet forces in April 1945, it was assigned to the RAF as the airhead of the British Zone of Berlin (along with Tegel in the French sector and Tempelhof in the US sector) and played a vital role in the 1948-49 Airlift. Its western boundary is within a few feet of the border between West Berlin and East Germany, the whole airfield being overlooked by Eastern bloc watch-towers. Two Chipmunks and a small RAF staff are the usual occupants for the routine tasks of exercising overflight rights and supporting and changing the Berlin Garrison. There are plans for rapidly and heavily reinforcing the station in a crisis. Also sharing accommodation here is 7 Flight of the Army Air Corps with Gazelle AH1s.

Gütersloh

Gütersloh is another ex-Luftwaffe base, opened in 1935 for a paratroop unit using Junkers Ju52s and later employed as a radar school and night fighter base. It was captured by US forces in 1945 and handed over to the RAF, which laid its first concrete runway in 1946. Army co-operation is the theme of Gütersloh today, the aerodrome being in the centre of the 1(BR) Corps area. Harriers plus Chinook and Puma helicopters are the current residents, assigned to fulfil the station's tasks of: (1) close support and reconnaissance; (2) short-range interdiction; (3) helicopter support; (4) air trooping and cargo handling; and (5) arrival base for troop reinforcements. There are 2,800 RAF personnel stationed at the aerodrome, plus 460 from the army, 450 civilian workers and 4,540 dependents. The army is responsible for generating many of Gütersloh's transport aircraft movements — RAF and civilian charter — the facilities typically handling over 100,000 passengers per year. (With the abnormal influx of 40,000 during Exercise 'Lionheart', the 1984 total was boosted to 158,432, together with 3,440 tonnes of freight.)

Originally, Wildenrath was the RAFG Harrier base, accepting No 4 Squadron in August 1970, followed by Nos 3 and 20. The last-mentioned had formed at Wittering on 1 October 1970 and moved to Wildenrath a few weeks later where it was officially constituted on 1 December. As part of a rationalisation programme of the Harrier force it disbanded on 28 February 1977 and transferred its aircraft to Nos 3 and 4 Squadrons, which were then on the move to Gütersloh. The last Harriers left the base on 4 April 1977. Each squadron has 16 Harriers — mostly GR3s, but including a couple of T4 two-seat trainers:

Squadron	Formed	Gütersloh	Codes
No 3	3 Jan 72 (Wildenrath)	Mar 77	AA-AZ
No 4	1 Jun 70 (Wittering)	4 Jan 77	A-Z

Right:
New colour schemes have been subjected to test on Harriers recently as a potential replacement for the standard overall green and grey disruptive markings. XV809 'AF' of No 3 Squadron is completely olive green, whilst XV738 'B' of No 4 Squadron is two tones of light grey. More commonly seen is winter camouflage in which the usual grey areas are replaced by white, as modelled by a No 4 Squadron Harrier T4 tandem-seat trainer.

Below:
Gütersloh's Harriers are flown by Nos 3 and 4 Squadrons, whose badges include a cockatrice and a sun divided by a flash of lightning.

Pumas arrived in RAFG during 1980 with No 230 Squadron from Odiham, which had been the second (and last) RAF squadron to receive the type — the first aircraft being delivered on 10 October 1971. Normally, some 15 are on strength. Transfer of the Pumas was made necessary by withdrawal of No 18 Squadron's Wessex HC2s on 1 December 1980 in preparation for the unit to re-equip with Chinook HC1s at Odiham. The first aircraft assigned to the squadron arrived at Odiham on 16 June 1981 and a new CO was appointed on 20 July. Officially re-formed on 24 February 1982, the new No 18 Squadron had its preparations for a return to RAFG disrupted by participation in the Falklands War which began two months later, and the follow-on requirement to base support helicopters on the islands. The first Chinooks did not arrive at Gütersloh until May 1983, when the first five, representing half the squadron, took up residence in a purpose-built hangar. The helicopter units are:

Squadron	Formed	Gütersloh	Codes
No 18	24 Feb 82	3 May 83	BA-BZ
No 230	Oct 71	14 Oct 80	DA-DZ

The base also houses the Rapier SAMs of No 63 Squadron, RAF Regiment, and is the HQ of the Regiment's No 33 Wing, which adminsters the airfield defence squadrons based in RAFG. Rapiers would still be required in wartime because of Gütersloh's role as a reinforcement base even after its Harriers and helicopters have left for the field sites.

Laarbruch

Like its sister strike/attack base, Brüggen, this aerodrome was built rapidly, but with considerable effort, near the Netherlands border during the early-1950s. The last RAF station constructed with war reparation moneys, Laarbuch opened in October 1954 after no less than 40,000 trees had been felled to clear its airfield, the present complement being 2,500 uniformed personnel and including those of four flying squadrons. Three are equipped with Tornado GR1s in the strike/attack role and the last operates Jaguar GR1s at present, but will be similarly equipped by the end of 1987. Until 1983 Laarbruch hosted two strike/attack units of Buccaneer S2Bs and its present recce/attack Jaguar-equipped No 2 Squadron.

Buccaneers had first arrived during January 1971 with No XV Squadron, whilst No 16 had begun receiving the same aircraft in June 1972 and officially re-formed in October. Tornados were delivered to XV Squadron from July 1983 as Buccaneer replacements, No 16 Squadron following suit soon afterwards. Completing the current trio, No 20 (Designate) Squadron began to work up with Tornados in spring 1984 — flying its first sortie on 2 May — and achieved operational status in June of that year when No 20 (Jaguar) Squadron disbanded at Brüggen. No 20 occupies a new complex of Mk 3 hardened shelters, work on which began in 1982 and was

No XV Squadron marks its Tornado GR1s in the range 'EA' to 'EZ' as part of an identification system covering both RAFG Tornado bases. By the end of 1986, seven squadrons will be using codes between 'AA' and 'GZ'.

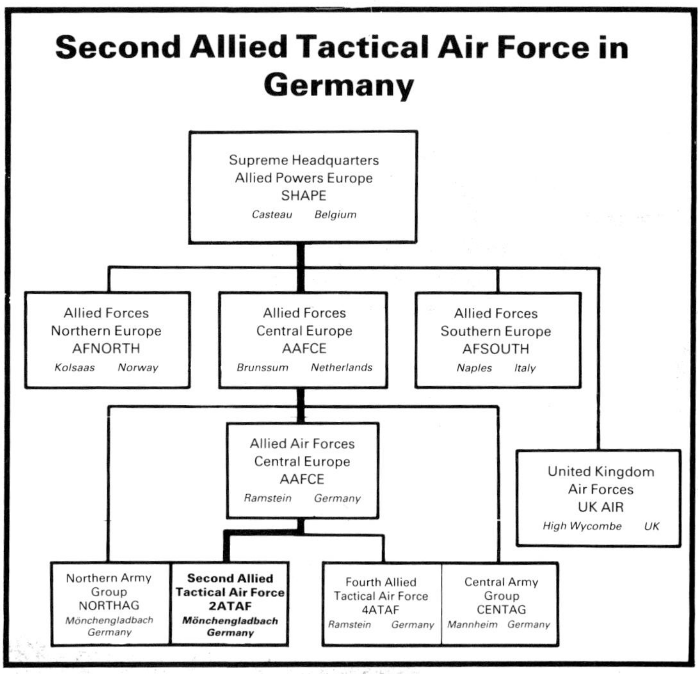

Laarbruch's three Tornado units are Nos XV, 16 and 20 Squadrons. The first-mentioned marks its aircraft 'XV', but the crossed keys and eagle badges of the other two squadrons are worn by their Tornados.
RAFG's last Jaguar GR1 unit still takes the style No II (Army Co-operation) Squadron on its badge and adorns its aircraft with a Wake knot.

DE

Overall:
Tornado GR1 ZD844/DE carrying the markings of No 31 Squadron, one of four former Jaguar units to fly the Tornado in RAF Germany.   Peter R. Foster

Right:
A Gütersloh-based Harrier GR3 of No 4 Squadron in its camouflaged hide.
Herman J. Sixma (IAAP)

Bottom:
A No 2 Squadron Jaguar GR1A based at RAF Laarbruch. The unit's last Jaguars will be replaced by a specialist recce model of the Tornado GR1 during 1987.
Herman J. Sixma (IAAP)

Above:
New accommodation has been built at Laarbruch for No 20 Squadron following its move from Brüggen to become the base's fourth resident. One of its Tornado GR1s is pictured taxying out through the trees from its Mk 3 HAS.

completed to basic standards in March 1984 (leaving the HPS and some other buildings to be finished over the following two years). The resident Tornado GR1 units are thus:

Squadron	First aircraft/date		Re-formed	Codes
No XV	ZA411	5 Jul 83	31 Oct 83	EA-EZ
No 16	ZA458	13 Dec 83	29 Feb 84	FA-FZ
No 20	ZA461	Mar 84	29 Jun 84	GA-GZ

Jaguars arrived at Laarbruch from February 1976 onwards to replace Phantom FGR2s, and No 2 Squadron was declared operational with the new equipment in the same October. Tasked with tactical reconnaissance and conventional attack, the Jaguars will be replaced by a specialist recce model of the Tornado GR1 during 1987. The last Jaguar is due to leave RAFG on 31 December 1987 and No 2 will be officially a Tornado unit from 1 January 1988 onwards. It remains to be seen which code letters No 2 adopts for its new aircraft. The Jaguars were originally coded with single letters so that when lined-up in the correct order they red 'SHINY TWOER JAG', but they now carry number identities. Some 18 aircraft are on charge, including two trainers, all of which have been fitted with updated navigation equipment to become Jaguar GR1As and T2As.

Squadron	First aircraft/date		Codes
No 2	XZ101	26 Feb 76	20-38

Further Laarbruch residents are No 26 Squadron, RAF Regiment, equipped with Rapier SAMs, and the light

armoured No 1 Squadron — the latter merely a lodger which is assigned to the Gütersloh Harriers in wartime. It is of interest that in July 1985 Laarbruch was the first RAFG station to be equipped with BRAMIS (Battle Readiness and Management Information System). This computerised and secure data net has terminal screens throughout the base, operating in a similar manner to national civilian schemes such as Ceefax and Oracle. BRAMIS comprises 999 totes with 99 pages each, on which can be displayed data on the functioning of the entire station — from individual aircraft weapon states to the location of police patrols.

Wildenrath

Completing the 'Clutch' bases — although it was the first to be built — Wildenrath was opened on 15 January 1952, initially as a fighter station. It now has five dispersal sites, of which three are HAS complexes. Strike-tasked Canberras were resident from 1956 until 1970, then Harriers up to 1977. The aerodrome then reverted to the fighter role with the arrival of Phantoms. Immediately prior to this, Lightnings had been responsible for policing the ADIZ, in the form of Nos 19 and 92 Squadrons at Gütersloh. These had flown out from Leconfield in September and December 1965, respectively, No 92 operating intitially from the fourth and most southern 'Clutch' base at Geilenkirchen until January 1968. (Geilenkirchen was then handed over to the German government and is now the HQ of NATO's force of 18 Boeing E-3A Sentry AWACS aircraft.) Phantom components of both squadrons formed at Wildenrath in 1976-77 and on their attainment of operational capability the Lightning units disbanded. The Phantom FGR2 squadrons

Right:
Training for the Phantom crews includes a yearly detachment to Akrotiri, Cyprus, for gunnery practice. Although this No 92 Squadron aircraft is fitted with Sky Flash and Sidewinder training rounds, the smoke trail confirms that its 20mm rotary cannon is in full working order.

26

TWOATAF HQ
Mönchengladbach

	BELGIUM Air Forces Command, (Evere)	**WEST GERMANY** Air Force Tactical Command (Cologne)	**NETHERLANDS** Tactical Air, Command (Ziest)	**UNITED KINGDOM** RAF Germany (Mönchengladbach)	**UNITED STATES** Air Force Europe (Ramstein)
Air Defence		F-4F Phantom: JG71, Wittmundhafen		Phantom FGR 2: 19/92 Sqns, Wildenrath	F-15C Eagle: 32 TFS, Soesterberg
	Nike-Hercules SAM: 9 Wing, Xanten Grefrath Thumberg Mulheim HAWK SAM: 43 Batt (Army) 62 Batt (Army)	Nike-Hercules SAM: FRR13, Soest FRR14, Oldenburg HAWK SAM: FRR3, Heide FRR4, Bremervörde	Nike-Hercules SAM: 118 Sqn Vorden 220 Sqn Schöppingen HAWK SAM: 324 Sqn Laatzen 326 Sqn Velmerstot 327 Sqn Goldbeck 328 Sqn Schwalenberg 500 Sqn Borstel 501 Sqn Winzlar 502 Sqn Hoysingshausen 503 Sqn Reinsdorf		
Offensive Operations	F-16A Falcon: 349/350 Sqns Bevekom 23/31 Sqns K. Brogel Mirage 5BA: 1/8Sqns Bierset 2 Sqn Florennes	Alpha Jet: JBG43, Oldenburg Tornado: JBG31, Norvenich F-4F Phantom: JBG36, Hopsten Pershing 1A SSM: FKG2, Geilenkirchen	NF-5A: 313/315 Sqn Twenthe 314 Sqn Eindhoven 316 Sqn Gilze-Rijen F-16A Falcon: 311/312 Sqns, Volkel 322/323 Sqn Leeuwarden	Harrier GR3: 3/4 Sqn Gütersloh Tornado GR1: 9/14/17/31 Sqns Brüggen 15/16/20 Sqns, Laarbruch	A-10A Thunderbolt: 78/91/92 TFS, Bentwaters F-111E: 55/77/79TFS, Upper Heyford
Reconnaissance	Mirage 5BR: 42 Sqn Florennes		F-16A (R) Falcon: 306 Sqn Volkel	Jaguar GR1: 2 Sqn Laarbruch	RF-4C Phantom: 1 TRS, Alconbury* Lockheed F-19 'Stealth': Alconbury/ Wethersfield?
Shorad			HAWK SAM/40L70 AAA: 119 Sqn Leeuwarden 121 Sqn Gilze-Rijen 221 Sqn Soesterberg 222 Sqn Twenthe 420 Sqn Volkel 421 Sqn de Peel 422 Sqn Eindhoven	Rapier SAM: 16 Sqn Wildenrath 26 Sqn Laarbruch 37 Sqn Brüggen 63 Sqns Gütersloh	

*To withdraw in 1987

Above:
In the hover — Chinook HC1 ZA720/BN of No 18 Squadron. The unit's first Chinooks arrived at RAF Gütersloh in May 1983.
P. A. Jackson

Below:
Tiger reflections — specially painted for a NATO Tiger Meet was Puma HC1 XW229/DB of No 230 Squadron.
Herman J. Sixma (IAAP)

have 12 or 13 aircraft each (carrying single letter codes, A-M for No 19; N-Z for No 92), and are:

Squadron	First aircraft/date		Re-formed	Operational
No 19	XV498 'J'	27 Sep 76	1 Oct 76	1 Jan 77
No 92	XV413 'Z'	2 Nov 76	1 Jan 77	1 Apr 77

Wildenrath's Pembrokes are flown by No 60 Squadron, which inherits the traditions of the 2nd TAF Communications Squadron, formed in 1944. RAF Germany Communications Squadron was re-titled No 60 in 1969 and initially complemented its Pembroke C1s with Devons, Herons (ex-Queen's Flight) and an Andover CC2. As the only RAF unit to fly regularly behind the Iron Curtain (on communications sorties to Berlin) it is equipped with the last seven Pembroke C1s in the RAF. Two of these were originally built for optional photo-survey roles and retain the designation C(PR)1.

Squadron	Formed	Codes
No 60	3 Feb 69 (from RAFGCS)	nil

In common with Gütersloh, Wildenrath is a major transit point for RAF and army personnel and equipment, and is additionally a Master Diversion Airfield available for emergency landings at any time. The Air Terminal is technically to full airport standard with customs and immigration services (provided by the RAF Police), plus money-changing facilities. A recent peak of activity was achieved in 1984 by the Air Movements Squadron when 20,899 troops engaged in Exercise 'Lionheart' increased the annual total to 74,506, plus 4,311 tons (4,380 tonnes) of freight. In addition, detachments temporarily assigned to other airfields handled 304 aircraft, representing 6,565 passengers, 132 tons (134 tonnes) of baggage and 957 tons (972 tonnes) of freight. Scheduled services at Wildenrath comprise two Britannia Airways Boeing 737s per week from Luton with personnel and families; and weekly flights by a No 115 Squadron Andover E3 for aeromedical evacuation to the UK; a Hercules to Decimonannu; a passenger and cargo VC10 to the same destination; and a Pembroke to Northolt. In addition, Pembrokes generate some three or four flights per day on RAFG communications flights.

Wildenrath also has the RAFG Freight Distribution Centre, which handles an average of 600 tons (610 tonnes) per month to keep RAFG stations operational. This is mainly from No 16 MU at Stafford via the daily sea-ferry trailer, but there is also some cargo airfreighted in from Brize Norton and Lyneham, plus items from No 11 MU at Chilmark (ordnance) and No 14 MU at Carlisle (avionics). The centre sorts and repackages equipment for onward transmission to the base and unit which originated the requirement. It is also involved in the tri-national Tornado programme and handles components produced by BAe at Preston for the German and Italian air force maintenance units at Erding and Novara, respectively. The station has its own railway spur from the German national system, but this is little used in day-to-day movement of supplies.

Completing Wildenrath's residents are the Rapier SAMs of No 16 Squadron; HQ No 4 Wing, which controls RAFG Rapier units; and four Gazelle AH1s of the Army Air Corps'

Above:
The fire station is one of Wildenrath's lesser-known features, but is of note in that it is the first new building of the type in RAFG. Opened on 3 May 1984 it has a crew of 34 RAF and 15 German personnel, and four vehicles. One of the two TFF Mk 9s (Truck, Fire-Fighting Mk 9) is drawn-up outside, with the domestic fire appliance on the right. The fourth tender is a TACR Mk 2 (Truck, Airfield Crash Rescue Mk 2) adaptation of the Range Rover.

Below:
The Freight Distribution Centre at Wildenrath is responsible for receiving supplies from the UK and forwarding them to the appropriate base in Germany. It is also an important component in the tri-national Tornado spares network.

12 Flight, assigned to liaison for HQ BAOR, plus RAFG, NORTHAG, AFCENT and RAF Wildenrath. One further army resident of note is No 21 Signal Regiment (Air Support), which formed on 5 March 1943 to provide radio communications for the 2nd TAF and continues in that role today with detachments at all RAFG bases. Its three principal components are 1 Squadron, providing BRUIN tactical communications in the rear combat zone for 1(BR) Corps, RAFG airfields and HQs and the Support Helicopter Force at Gütersloh and in the field; 2 Squadron assigned to the Harrier Force at Gütersloh and its field deployments; and 3 Squadron, maintaining telephone lines to the four airfields, operating the Station Radio Relay Network (STARRNET) between RAFG bases, and linking British Forces Germany with the UK. Some 20% of military personnel on the station are army.

Many units, functions and aspects are common to all RAFG stations — not least basic layout and design of buildings at the 'Clutch' aerodromes. The usual airfield configuration is an east-west runway some 8,100ft in length (Gütersloh is 7,400ft)

with around 7½-9 miles (12-15km) of perimeter fence to be guarded. In fact bases have three runways available in wartime, because there are two parallel taxiways at each which are available as full-length, half-width strips if the main is put out of action.

However, great pains have been taken to keep RAFG flying in the event of air and sabotage attacks on its stations. Dispersed around the airfields are groups of hardened aircraft shelters (HAS), one 'farm' of which is assigned to each operational squadron. Capable of resisting a direct hit by a 1,000lb (454kg) bomb, these miniature hangars are so arranged that no more than two are in a straight line in each group. German bases were the first in the RAF to have the HAS, and so feature the Mk 1 design with its outward-swinging hinged doors. Where expansion is taking place — such as at Laarbruch — the new Mk 3 HAS is being added. Mk 3s are larger, have an 'Aerospace Ground Annexe' (a glorified name for a hardened lean-to for storing ground equipment), and doors rolling on wheels. When fitted with an annexe and other improvements the old HAS becomes a 'Modified Mk 1' but can still take only one Tornado, two Jaguars or three tightly-packed Harriers. Mk 3s will easily take two Tornados.

Because the HAS doors must be open to launch and recover aircraft (they taxi-out under their own power, and are pulled inside backwards by a power winch), no pretence can be made at proofing against NBC contamination. Similarly, the Hardened Equipment Shelters (HES) included in each HAS farm for storing fuel bowsers and other large items are also unprotected. In wartime, therefore, aircraft turn-round and maintenance will have to be conducted in the confines of the HAS (as in peacetime) with the additional encumbrance of an NBC protective suit.

Contaminated clothing can be discarded when entering other buildings with a filtered air supply. Each strike/attack unit has a Personnel Briefing Facility (called a Pilot BF in the days of the single-seat Jaguar) which is its Squadron HQ for flight-planning and the other administrative tasks needed to keep it operative. Hardened Personnel Shelters are equipped with bunk beds and very restricted free space for off-duty aerodrome staff of all grades, these being the only reinforced buildings not used in peacetime. The base commander and his aides direct their war from the Combat Operations Centre, which is a standard HAS without large doors, divided horizontally to have an upper floor.

Within are the familiar 'tote boards' showing the status of each aircraft on the base and the planned sorties for the day, plus other departments, including the Ground Defence Operations Centre. GDOC personnel co-ordinate the actions and observations of the RAF Regiment SAM and armoured

Top:
Most of RAFG's Hardened Aircraft Shelters are of the Mk 1 type with hinged, bulged doors which, when open, remain beneath a continuation of the roof. This example, at Laarbruch, has been built at the entrance to a revetment once used by Canberras. It has also been updated to Modified Mk 1 standard with the addition of an Aerospace Ground Annexe on the right for equipment storage.

Above:
The Mk 3 HAS is a larger shelter than the Mk 1, capable of holding two Tornados. New Mk 3s have been built at Brüggen and Laarbruch, their most obvious features being the flat doors which are rolled back on wheels for aircraft to pass. A large equipment annexe is standard.

defence squadrons and ensure rapid reaction by specialist teams to emergencies such as fire, contamination and infiltration. It is to the Combat Operations Centre (COC) of strike/attack bases that TWOATAF signals its instructions for a raid to be mounted, specifying the target and number of aircraft. The base commander will nominate the squadron(s) to be sent, taking into account factors such as experience, specialisation and the current state of aircraft. A telebrief landline connects each HAS to the COC.

Combat elements controlled by each station will be expanded during TTW by reinforcements from the UK — provided by the OCUs, in the case of aircraft. The one exception is Wildenrath, which will augment its interceptor forces with a squadron of USAF F-4 Phantoms. (Other RAF stations may be designated as bases for aircraft arriving from the US, but this has not been made public.) At Gütersloh, No 233 OCU from Wittering would add some 12 Harriers to the resident squadrons, and No 240 OCU's Pumas and Chinooks would arrive from Odiham to bolster the Support Helicopter Force. It is possible that Brüggen might renew its associations with the Jaguar by taking in aircraft and pilots of Lossiemouth-based No 226 OCU, whilst from the same base, Buccaneers of No 237 OCU could be allocated to Laarbruch to operate in the Pave Way/Pave Spike laser-guided bombing role. Finally, a mention must be made of the Gazelle HT3s, of No 2 FTS at Shawbury which would be allocated in pairs to each station, probably with the addition of some extras to TWOATAF's war HQ for courier duties. Their red-and-white training colours exchanged for camouflage, the Gazelles would take a video cameraman aloft immediately after an air raid to survey the damage so that repair priorities can be assessed.

Ground forces from both the RAF Regiment and army will make haste to RAFG from their peacetime bases in an emergency, the former to be taken in hand by No 33 Wing at Gütersloh. There will be an eventual total of six Regiment squadrons operating in the light armoured role with their Scorpion vehicles for air base defence, two of them assigned to the Harrier Force. Of these only No 1 Squadron is based in-theatre, at Laarbruch, the other being No 2, which will come from Hullavington. No 15 Squadron, also at Hullavington, is assigned to Wildenrath; whilst Nos 51 and 58 Squadrons from Catterick go to Brüggen and Laarbruch respectively. If possible, No 34 Field Squadron will leave its

Above:
The 'tone-down' procedure for aerodromes to make them less visible from the air includes the covering of concrete (including shelters) with a chemical which has a rusty brown colour (there are other, indelicate descriptions!). Following the relaying of a hardstanding at Wildenrath, a tractor equipped with agricultural spray-bars is applying the tone-down chemical.

Land Rovers at Akrotiri, Cyprus, and travel to Germany to collect stock-piled armour for an undisclosed role. The helicopter elements only qualify for the Land Rovers and rifles of a Field Squadron, this being made-up from the Training Support Flight at RAF Catterick and the otherwise ceremonial personnel of the Queen's Colour Squadron from RAF Uxbridge.

Army support comes from the Royal Engineers, principally in the form of airfield repair services. A slightly different situation again obtains for the units which will leave Gütersloh for dispersed operations, and in the case of the Harriers, the Germany-resident 10 Field Squadron will be complemented by UK-based 48 Field Squadron in the task of preparing and maintaining sites. Chinook and Puma detachment bases are similarly the responsibility of 11 and 32 Field Squadrons. Piles of aggregate and quick-drying cement, rolls of aluminium matting, roadrollers, dumper trucks and the like will be found stockpiled at Brüggen, Laarbruch and Wildenrath awaiting the arrival of 52, 50 and 53 Field Squadrons (Construction), respectively, with about 120 men each. These regularly spend their annual training periods in Germany, blowing 15ft deep 'bomb' craters in taxiways and then repairing the damage.

RAF Regiment in Germany

Since its formation in 1942, the RAF Regiment has been responsible for defending aerodromes and thus keeping the RAF flying in wartime. Major units based in, or assigned to, Germany have one of two functions: Low-Level Air Defence (LLAD) with BAeD Rapier short-range SAMs; and defence against surface forces. For the latter function there are both Light Armoured Squadrons with tracked vehicles, and Field Squadrons with 'soft-skinned' Land Rovers.

RAFG's four LLAD squadrons constitute No 4 Wing at Wildenrath (this unit additionally responsible for basic Rapier operator training for the whole RAF). The Wing inherits the traditions of No 1304 Wing which first came to Europe on D-Day, but its present commission began at Catterick in December 1973, just before transfer to RAFG. It has been at Wildenrath since July 1978. Individual components are:

No 16 Squadron, Wildenrath: Re-formed with Rapier at North Luffenham, August 1975; transferred to Wildenrath, February 1976.

Below:
The badge of the RAF Regiment.

A Rapier fire unit ready for action. Two of the eight-man team attached to each fire unit are constantly on duty, comprising the NCO Tactical Controller (standing) and airman Operator. Marconi DN181 Blindfire radar is in the foreground, with the four-round launcher at the rear. Optical tracking equipment is included in the firing position. Rapier will constantly search for targets and interrogate their IFF, but the Tactical Controller can instantly realign the system on to a target acquired visually.

Below:
No 4 Wing, RAF Regiment, based at Wildenrath, comprises Nos 16, 26, 37 and 63 Squadrons equipped with Rapier SAMs.

No 26 Squadron, Laarbruch: Re-formed in situ at Laarbruch with Rapiers, April 1976, by renumbering of No 58 Squadron. First British Forces Germany Rapier unit equipped with Blindfire, May 1979.

No 37 Squadron, Brüggen: Re-formed on Rapier and installed at Brüggen, 1 April 1976.

No 63 Squadron, Gütersloh: First Regiment Rapier unit. Installed at Gütersloh, July 1974.

Rapier units all have the same basic structure. Squadrons, which are commanded by a Flying Officer or Pilot Officer, comprise four Flights: HQ, Engineering, and two Rapier Flights, with each of the last-mentioned having four Fire Units. Intended to operate autonomously, a Fire Unit comprises one launch trailer (mounting four missiles at a time), the optical tracking equipment, DN181 Blindfire radar, camping equipment, three Land Rovers, and eight personnel (a sergeant, two corporals and five men). A squadron's eight Fire Units are kept serviceable by the four travelling Forward Rapier Teams attached to the Engineering Flight for first-line maintenance, and any defective modules are brought back to the Flight's group of four-tonne trucks which form a mobile workshop.

Squadrons' higher command is more complex. As air defence units they are under constant NATO operational command via No 4 Wing, although administration and discipline are a responsibility of their host station, and HQ RAFG supplies engineering support directly. The exceptions are Nos 16 and 37 Squadrons, which are jointly administered by No 4 Wing, instead of the Wildenrath and Brüggen station commanders.

Each year, squadrons deploy for one month at South Uist, Hebrides, on live firing practice, and on a rotational basis are called upon to spend four months in the Falklands Islands manning defences there, where a live launch is also conducted. However, from 1985 onwards (it was officially opened on 29 May), Wildenrath has had the services of a GQ Defence Systems Ltd Air Defence Tactical Training Theatre (ADT3 for short). Functioning like a planetarium, the ADT3 provides highly realistic, computerised exercise scenarios in which the two-man Rapier operating team of Tactical Controller and Operator can receive continuation training. Positioned with

Left:

Rapier launching. Fire units are positioned a mile or two from their parent airfield on sites which command an unobstructed field of fire. No other preparation is required, whereas this launch is at a range with concrete emplacements.

Below:

No 33 Wing, RAF Regiment, at Gütersloh, controls only Laarbruch-based No 1 Squadron in peacetime.

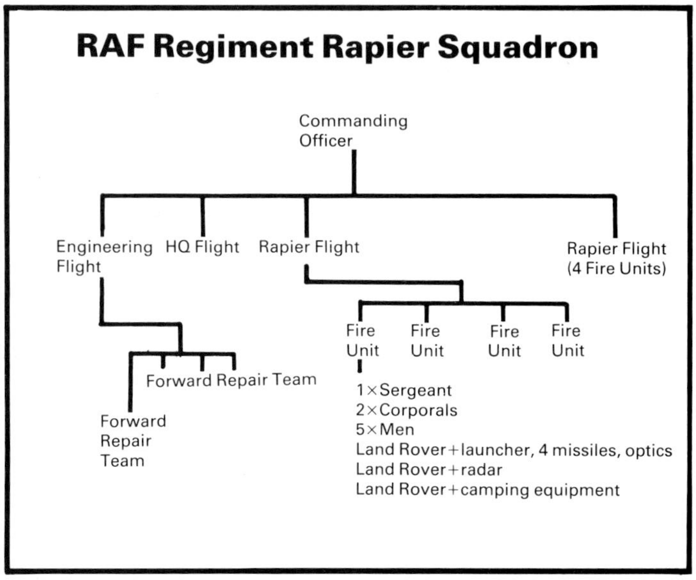

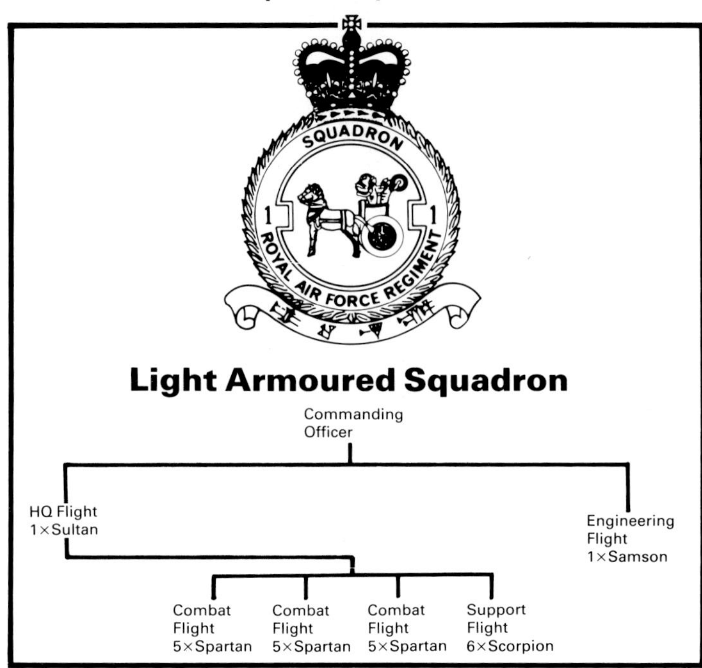

Light Armoured Squadron

Below:

Looking like a planetarium from the outside — and operating on a similar principle within — the ADT3 dome at Wildenrath trains Rapier operators in a highly realistic environment at a fraction of the cost of full-scale practice. Developed by GQ Defence Systems in the remarkably short period of two years, the system is being installed additionally at Lossiemouth and West Raynham, whilst the army will have its own at Dortmund and Larkhill.

the fire unit in the centre of the dome, the crew sees a 360°
horizon produced by 24 slide projectors. In addition, targets
are generated by four further projectors, each with a
repertoire of 50 aircraft operational profiles which can be
applied to any make of aircraft of which a model has been
pre-filmed. Images of friend and foe move around the walls of
the dome, banking and turning realistically to a background of
aircraft noise (plus battle sounds, if desired). A simulated
missile launch, if judged successful by the computer driving the
whole system, produces a satisfying fireball and disappearance
of the target, all engagements being recorded on video tape for
debriefing.

ADT3 reproduces the Rapier's warning sounds in its
Operator's headset, these comprising the Alarm (aircraft
located), Taboo (missiles directed towards a designated 'safe
area'), Fault, and Late IFF return. Although Rapier
automatically locks on to targets if they do not immediately
return an IFF signal, the Tactical Controller can also instantly
realign the system by his 'pointing stick'. Appearing to be no
more than a wooden pistol mounted on a pole, this over-rides
the radar and directs the Operator's optical tracker towards a
target acquired visually. Therefore the simple pointing stick
can defeat an intruder who has managed to mask his approach
by sophisticated electronic jamming.

Regiment ground units fall under No 33 Wing, which moved
to Germany in June 1973, initially at Wildenrath. Transferred
to Laarbruch in March 1976, No 33 assumed its current
position at Gütersloh in August 1980 with prime responsibility
for defence of the Harrier Force. Its sole German-based unit
is:

No 1 Squadron, Laarbruch: Tracing its origins back to No 1
Armoured Car Company, formed at Heliopolis, Egypt, in
1921, the unit came to Germany in August 1970 as a Field
Squadron and began to re-equip with light armoured vehicles
on 8 April 1982, being declared operational in May 1983. Its
first action on being called to service would be to cross the
Rhine to meet up with Harrier detachments in the field.

Four UK-based Light Armoured Squadrons are assigned to
wartime reinforcement of RAFG: No 2 ex-Hullavington (No 5
Wing), also to Gütersloh; No 15 ex-Hullavington (No 5 Wing)
to Wildenrath; No 51 ex-Catterick (No 3 Wing) to Brüggen;
and No 58 ex-Catterick (No 3 Wing) to Laarbruch. In addition
— and if circumstances permit — No 34 Field Squadron from
Akrotiri, Cyprus, will transfer to Germany and collect
stockpiled armour on arrival. Each squadron comprises 162
personnel (including seven officers) and 23 NBC-proof
vehicles of four types — all based on the same Alvis chassis —
divided into six Flights. The HQ Flight is formed around a
single FV105 Sultan command post, whilst the Engineering
Flight has one FV106 Samson recovery vehicle. Three Combat
Flights each have five FV103 Spartan armoured personnel
carriers, each holding five troops plus the two-man crew.
Finally, a Support Weapons Flight is equipped with six FV101
Scorpion fire support vehicles mounting a 76mm gun and
7.62mm machine gun. Direct fire range of the former is
2,200m, and indirect fire 5,000m.

Troops are armed with machine guns and the new LAW 80
anti-tank projectile, as are those of the Queen's Colour
Squadron (QCS) from Uxbridge and Training Support Flight,
Catterick, who are Land Rover-mobile in defence of the
Support Helicopter Force. It was the QCS which, in October
1985, was the first RAF unit to be issued with SA80 Endeavour
5.56mm rifles, eventually to be used by all branches of the
armed forces. Regiment personnel train the ancillary staff who
take up arms in an emergency (from 1 April 1984 all WAAFs
have had to qualify on the rifle range for base defence), but the
policy of sub-contracting accountancy, catering and other
services to civilian firms is reducing the number of personnel
available.

Below:

**In a typical operational environment, defending Harriers in the
field, are vehicles of No 1 Squadron. Principal equipment of a
Light Armoured Squadron comprises FV103 Spartan armoured
personnel carriers (left) and FV101 Scorpion fire support vehicles
— the latter mounting a 76mm gun.**

No 431 Maintenance Unit

Based at Brüggen, although reporting directly to HQ RAFG, No 431 MU assumed its present form in 1966 with the amalgamation of the original No 431 MU supply depot, No 420 MU at Laarbruch (Aircraft Engineering Repair & Salvage Unit), and the Forward Repair Unit at Butzweilerhof (motor transport servicing and general engineering). The Brüggen site occupies 38 acres (15.4 hectares) on the northwest corner of the aerodrome, and includes 30 storage sheds, 25 workshops, a high-density storage hangar and outside storage areas. Hangarage and engine test facilities are also employed on the airfield, and a detachment works at the army's nearby 3 Base Ammunition Depot, part of which is used to store RAF conventional ordnance.

No 431 MU is organised into four squadrons, which are the:

Aircraft Engineering Section handling Cat 3 aircraft repairs and modification programmes, aircraft component repair, salvage of crashed aircraft, battle damage repair, and other minor tasks. Between 50% and 66% of aircraft work is undertaken away from Brüggen, and up to 15 aircraft can be receiving attention at one time.

Propulsion Squadron for the repair of RB199 (Tornado) and Adour (Jaguar) engine modules and jetpipes; and fault diagnosis, rectification and test of RB199, Adour and Spey (Phantom). The Pegasus (Harrier) facility in RAFG is at Gütersloh's ASF.

Mechanical Engineering Ground Squadron responsible for freight distribution, second line MT servicing and support, and general engineering support. The last-mentioned extends to manufacture of some items of aircraft primary structure, for which the unit is licensed by BAe/Panavia, and such local modification items as (for example) a Sidewinder AAM adaptor for Jaguars.

Supply Squadron which maintains war and contingency stocks; and receives, stores and issues vehicles and explosives.

The MU acts as a development and teaching unit for techniques of aircraft battle damage repair (BDR), interchanging knowledge with other air forces. Four instructors and an NCO handle this vital task, liaising also with the BDR co-ordinator on each aerodrome. BDR aims to return combat-damaged aircraft to service in 8-12 hours in place of a repair which would in peacetime take weeks or months, and possibly include the supply of replacement parts from the maker. Each job presents a new challenge, the only firm rule being that the aircraft should be safe to fly afterwards — although externally applied metal patching plates over shell holes would obviously result in slight changes of trim! Realistic BDR training during exercises involves a referee declaring a Tornado or Jaguar to be out of use until repair personnel have rectified damage to a trolley-mounted section of some long-since scrapped aircraft. Imaginative repair of damaged control rods, parted electric wiring and similar damage will immensely increase the number of RAFG aircraft ready for combat on the second and subsequent days of any war.

Above:
No 431 MU handles all Category 3 aircraft repairs and modifications within RAF Germany, over half of such work normally being undertaken away from its base at Brüggen. The Jaguar commitment has been greatly reduced since 1984 but will not end until 1987.

Below:
The badge of No 431 Maintenance Unit.

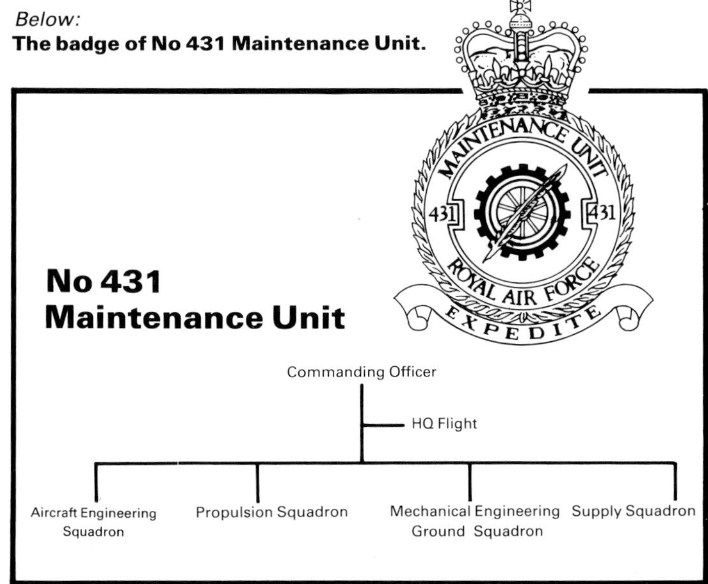

4. WEAPONRY

Throughout the world, combat aircraft are only as good as the weapons they carry and it is therefore incumbent upon any air force which has acquired the best aircraft also to fit it with armament equal to its potential. There can be little doubt that this has been done in RAF Germany, where some of the West's most capable and versatile aircraft are based. Naturally, this chapter will begin with a description of the Tornado's considerable warload, but interceptor and reconnaissance equipment also deserves mention, as does the support effort involved in keeping RAFG's aircraft in flying trim.

From the outset, the interdictor Tornado was designed to be compatible with a broad spectrum of NATO air weapons, in addition to having a pair of newly-designed IWKA-Mauser 27mm cannon mounted internally. Other offensive equipment is carried on the three under-fuselage pylons (centreline and two 'shoulder'), leaving the wing pylons free for defensive equipment and fuel tanks. In the strike role, the Tornado GR1 will carry a single nuclear weapon — reported by unofficial, civilian sources to be a 950lb (431kg) device which has a variable yield of up to 500 kilotons and is based on the American B61 design.

Matching the incredible precision of its navigation system, the Tornado can carry a single Mk 13/15 laser-guided bomb (LGB) of 1,380lb (626kg) on each of the three under-fuselage carriers, although it will have to rely on another aircraft or ground source to provide target illumination. When carrying the Mk 13/1 free-fall bomb — usually fitted with a retarding tail to prevent rebounding when dropped from ultra-low level — it is possible to increase the load to eight, arranged as tandem pairs on the shoulder pylons, with the option of a 330gal (1,500 litre) fuel drop tank on the centreline. RAFG has no dedicated tanker support, so Tornados are not fitted with the optional FR probe seen on many UK-based aircraft.

Introduced to RAFG in 1985 for the important counter-air role, the Hunting JP233 is a 5,148lb (2,335kg) pannier carried in pairs beneath the fuselage, each containing 30 SG357 parachute-retarded runway-cratering munitions and 215 HB875 area denial mines to delay the repair process. A typical

Above:
A primary defensive aid for the Tornado is its Philips BOZ-107 chaff/flare pod which is carried on the starboard outer wing pylon, but seen here during servicing at Brüggen. Flare cartridges are fired from the rear to confuse heat-seeking missiles, whilst metallic needles of chaff (World War 2 'Window') are ejected from the forward edge of the black band.

Below:
Tornado servicing at Brüggen is undertaken in a refurbished hangar which has electric, air and hydraulic mains plumbed into the floor for a safer, cleaner and quieter environment. Note how the windscreen hinges forward for access.

JP233 attack would be made at 200ft (61m) and 500kt (927km/hr), with the bomblets being released at one of two rates, depending upon whether the aircraft is flying along or across the enemy runway. Immediately thereafter the empty panniers are jettisoned to improve aircraft performance. In the case of attacks against battlefield targets, Tornados will use the newly improved version of the Hunting BL755 Cluster Bomb Unit (CBU), with its greater capability against the armour of main battle tanks. Standard BL755s remain in widespread use with the RAF, however, each weighing 610lb (277kg) and occupying about the same volume as a 1,000lb bomb (ie, up to eight may be carried by the Tornado).

Assisting the Tornado to undertake its mission successfully are defensive aids ranged on the wing pylons. Marconi's ARI 23246/1 Sky Shadow automatic, programmable jammer pod is located outboard on the port side, whilst the starboard outer holds a Philips BOZ-107 chaff/flare dispenser. These installations work independently of each other, the BOZ being operated manually. Inboard pylons, carrying a 330gal (1,500 litre) fuel tank, mount a self-defence AIM-9L Sidewinder AAM on an auxiliary carrier attached to the side nearest the fuselage. From 1987 onwards the newly-developed BAe Alarm (Air-Launched Anti-Radiation Missile) is scheduled to become available for fitment to the outer side of the same pylon to knock out enemy radars. A larger load of Alarms may be carried for a dedicated anti-radar mission — possibly as many as seven if Sidewinders are omitted.

In 1988, when No 2 Squadron becomes operational with reconnaissance Tornados, it will have what is claimed to be the most advanced tactical sensor system in the world. The new equipment, which began flight-testing in 1985, dispenses with the traditional film-negative camera in favour of a sideways-looking infra-red (SLIR) system and BAe Linescan 4000 IR surveillance equipment. Both sensors are mounted in the cannon bays, SLIR looking through a small window in the fuselage sides, whilst the Linescan viewer is accommodated in a belly fairing immediately behind the LRMTS laser ranger housing. Information will be recorded solely on video tape for later play-back, with enhancement and magnification options available for more detailed study of important features.

A new aircraft has brought new servicing facilities in its wake. At Brüggen, the Aircraft Servicing Flight, which comprises 115 men of various trades, assumed responsibility for Minor Servicing of the Tornado in July 1985, having had its hangar extensively modified. Most noticeable is the lack of wires and leads littering the floor, because each working position now has electricity, compressed air and hydraulic points installed at ground level to give a quieter, more efficient environment. The Flight has been responsible for acceptance checks taking between five and 20 working days on newly-arrived Tornados, and with the 'Minor' commitment it will see the aircraft every 300 flying hours for a 25-day programme of mods incorporation and corrosion/fatigue inspection. Every 1,200 hours the aircraft are ferried to St Athan for Major Servicing.

The Tornado programme being almost complete, RAFG's next major aircraft programme is replacement of the Harrier GR3 by its Anglo-American cousin the GR5 (alias AV-8B

Harrier II). Stationed at Gütersloh with Nos 3 and 4 Squadrons, the existing aircraft operate in the close support role with 1,000lb (454kg) bombs — in laser-guided or parachute-retarded form — BL755 CBUs and the two ADEN 30mm cannon fitted in flush, under-fuselage pods. No 4 Squadron operates only with CBUs and cannon, being instead given a 40% tactical reconnaissance commitment with a centreline pod containing four 70mm F95 Mk 7 cameras and one 5in (127mm) F135. (All Harriers, it will be recalled, have an oblique, left-facing F95 in the forward fuselage.)

Two or four CBUs or bombs are usually carried under the wings, depending upon whether or not the 100gal (455 litre) drop-tanks are fitted to the inboard pair for increased range. With gun pods attached it is possible to have a further bomb or tank on the centreline, although the aircraft in RAFG are no longer issued with MATRA 68mm SNEB rocket pods. The defensive fit on Harrier GR3s includes an AIM-9L Sidewinder AAM and a Philips-MATRA Phimat flare dispenser. However, as the proposed Phase 6 modification for the aircraft has been cancelled (in view of the GR5's imminence), wingtip Sidewinder rails have not been fitted, so self-protection equipment takes up valuable weapon space. A few Harriers modified for the Falklands war have a Tracor AN/ALE-40 chaff/flare dispenser in the lower rear fuselage, the rest having to make do with chaff stuffed in the airbrake for a 'one time shot' against missile guidance radars which have locked on.

ALE-40 is but one of the many 'extras' to be available as standard from 1987 onwards when the first of the RAF's initial 60 Harrier GR5s is delivered to Gütersloh. The second-generation aircraft has wing pylons increased from four to eight in recognition of the fact that it will be capable of carrying twice the weapon load of its predecessor. Other new features will include an uprated Rolls-Royce Pegasus engine, internal Marconi Zeus ECM equipment, a Ferranti FIN 1075 INS, twin ADEN 25mm cannon and a panoramic camera in the nose. The first of two pre-series GR5s flew on 30 April 1985, and unlike the US Marine Corps the RAF does not propose at this stage to order a two-seat trainer version to replace the Harrier T4. A typical warload for the GR5 will be seven CBUs, two Sidewinders and the cannon.

The Jaguar now remains in RAFG only for reconnaissance, following the conversion of No 14 Squadron to Tornados in November 1985. The sole operator in the Command, No 2

Above:
Bombing-up a Harrier GR3 for a short-range sortie with Hunting BL755 cluster bombs on each of the four underwing pylons. BL755 scatters 147 bomblets over the target area, each capable of penetrating armour up to 250mm. An improved version of the weapon is entering service.

Below:
Harrier GR3s of No 4 Squadron fly in formation at low level over Germany. The two aircraft nearest the camera carry reconnaissance pods to represent the unit's partial dedication to this role.

Squadron, will not dispose of its Jaguars until the end of 1987, longer life being ensured in part by their use in the recce regime, which notches up the fatigue 'points' at a slower rate than strike/attack training. Futher service extension moves have involved the incorporation of Mod 1114: Ferranti FIN 1064 inertial nav/attack equipment, all aircraft having been so updated by the ASF at Brüggen or at RAF Abingdon by mid-1985, raising their designation to Jaguar GR1A (and T2A). Brüggen ASF has retained the RAFG Jaguar servicing capability even though No 2 Squadron is based at Laarbruch.

Standard Jaguar equipment is a BAe (formerly BAC) centreline recce pod weighing some 1,000lb (500kg) and containing a fan of four F95 Mk 10 cameras (capable of taking up to 12 pictures per second each); a forward-facing F95 Mk 7; and a downward pointing IR linescan unit which may be replaced with an F126 optical camera, if so desired. The four

Mk 10s provide complete horizon-to-horizon coverage (195° in fact), with a slight overlap to compensate for the fact that the outer pair have a 3in lens, compared to 1.5in for those recording the ground closer to the aircraft. Linescan has a 120° field of view (mapping a 870ft strip when flying at 250ft) and can be stabilised automatically to compensate for up to 30° of aircraft roll or slewed up to 30° to either side. The fixed F126 has a more restricted 74° field. Two internal ADEN 30mm cannon are complemented on armed reconnaissances by a BL755 CBU on each outer pylon, leaving the inboard units to carry a 264gal (1,200 litre) drop-tank. Self-protection measures include AIM-9L Sidewinders, Phimat chaff dispensers and a Westinghouse AN/ALQ-101-10 jamming pod — but obviously not all at once, if only the CBUs are dispensed with. A typical fit would be Phimat in the starboard outer position, with an ALQ-101 on the opposite side, complemented by a Tracor flare dispenser in the drogue-chute housing.

There is no 'either-or' situation with the Phantom FGR2 air defence fighter, which carries a formidable array of four BAe Sky Flash and four AIM-9AL Sidewinder AAMs, plus a cannon pod. Sky Flash, which replaced the similar-sized AIM-7E2 Sparrow in RAFG from January 1981, is a semi-active radar guided weapon with a range of up to 25 miles (40km). AIM-9L is an infra-red guided weapon which arrived in RAFG soon after the Sky Flash as a substitute for AIM-9Gs. Produced in a European consortium led by Bodenseewerk, the -9L has a range of some 11 miles (18km).

Prime sensor in the Phantom is its Ferranti AWG-12 pulse-Doppler radar weapon system. Evolved to British requirements from the Westinghouse AN/AWG-10, this look-down radar has undergone a recent update programme which has doubled the mean time between component failures, improved jamming resistance and extended its operational envelope. In addition, the cannon aiming sight has been optimised for air-to-air roles instead of ground attack. With these modifications the Phantom will remain in service with RAFG for perhaps a decade or more until the embryo European fighter, probably based on the BAe EAP, is fully developed.

Unusually, the Phantom carries its external fuel on the outboard wing attachments in two 310gal (1,410 litre) tanks, whilst it is the inboard pylons which each carry a pair of Sidewinders. The Sky Flashes are semi-recessed in the belly, and the cannon pod occupies the centreline position. Phantom FGR2s use the General Electric SUU-23/A pod containing a GAU-4 Vulcan 20mm six-barrel rotary cannon, firing at the rate of up to 6,000 rounds per minute. Its weight, fully loaded with 1,200 rounds, is 1,780lb (807kg).

Phantom maintenance tasks are assigned to Wildenrath's Aircraft Servicing Flight, where a team of 54 men, aided by specialists as required, work on two aircraft at a time. Every 125 flying hours, squadrons conduct the Primary check, but the aircraft goes into the ASF for its Primary Star servicing at 250 hours (increased in 1984 from 200 hours), which takes 12 days. Minor, Minor Star and Major works follow at 500, 1,000 and 2,000 hours, the more involved tasks requiring return to the UK. Most Phantoms in RAFG have flown between 3,000 and 4,000 hours. In parallel with the counting of hours, strain gauges mounted in the aircraft tot up fatigue on a points basis,

with a score of 60 requiring a visit to the RAF Engineering Wing at St Athan, and 100 resulting in return to BAe at Brough to be 'zeroed' with the appropriate replacement and strengthening actions.

Not all of RAFG's aircraft require weapons to execute their tasks, as evidenced by the Support Helicopter Force at Gütersloh. Whilst the Puma HC1 has provision for a light machine gun in the cabin doorway, this is rarely fitted for the task of transporting army personnel and equipment. The more normal fitment, on the starboard side, is a winch, suitable for loads the weight of two human beings. All Pumas are now fitted with the French-designed 'polyvalent' air intake filters to guard against foreign object ingestion, although the sand-filtering option is not employed. These guards increase fuel consumption by 2% — or 5% if anti-icing is selected — the Puma not being cleared for peacetime flying in falling snow or with visibility under 1,000m (1,100yd). Chinooks too can position a 7.62mm machine gun in the forward, starboard doorway, but seldom do so.

Both helicopter types are maintained at their home base by the local Aircraft Engineering Servicing Flight, where all mechanical components of Puma, Chinook and Harrier are catered for. One of the more common tasks for the 70-man team here is rectifying fine particle erosion on the leading edge of fibre composite rotor blades, but other work includes stripping and re-building rotor heads, and deep stripping of Turbomeca Turmo (Puma) and Avco-Lycoming T55 (Chinook) engines. Harrier services involve overhaul of the Pegasus vectored thrust turbofan, the AESF even re-assembling the compressor on the basis of blade-balancing data supplied for each set of components by Rolls-Royce's computer back in the UK.

Logically, Wildenrath is the RAF's centre for Pembroke maintenance, only the Leonides engines going to Alvis for overhaul under a contract negotiated yearly. Having been re-sparred in the early-1970s, the aircraft are exceptionally corrosion-free and, with the exception of engines, are easy to maintain. Primary servicing is a four-hour task undertaken after every 60 hours of flight, followed by Primary Star, Minor and Minor Star at 120, 240 and 480 hours, then Major Servicing at 960 hours — this taking 26-28 days of work. Aircraft utilisation is around 500 hours per year, those at Wildenrath having accumulated individual totals of between 5,150 and 8,950 hours by 1985.

At present rates the venerable Pembrokes will be able to remain in service until 1991, and may well do so despite rumours of replacement by ex-Queen's Flight Andovers and even BAe125s. No 60 has eight navigators and seven pilots, and is responsible for converting its own new personnel to the Pembroke. There were four 'positively the last' crew conversion courses over a 30-month period in 1983-84, and personnel are convinced that there will be several more before the description is applied accurately. All aircraft have dual control, but are manned by a pilot and navigator alone, the pilot doing the flying and the navigator everything else. In unique units such as No 60 there is a unique fund of experience — borne out by the fact that pilots' ages range between 25 and 53. Having been built from 1953 onwards, some of the Pembrokes are thus older than the men who fly them, and the only concession to the 1980s is installation of Decca navigation equipment.

Above:
Regular exercises at station, Command and NATO level ensure that RAFG can come to combat readiness within a matter of hours. Taxying out of its HAS for a practice take-off is a Tornado GR1 of No 17 Squadron, Brüggen.

Below:
Changing a Harrier's Pegasus engine during a field deployment permits little protection from the elements.

Few of the RAF's units practise their war roles as regularly as those based in Germany. As was explained in an earlier chapter, some cannot help but do so because their daily operations are mounted from the hardened accommodation built for wartime use. For others, realistic training requires a visit to the German countryside for off-airfield operations.

The Tornado squadrons will fight from their normal bases. Defended by the RAF Regiment and other armed personnel, Brüggen and Laarbruch will launch their strike/attack missions from the parallel taxiways if the main runway is put out of action. Even then, the full length of concrete will not be needed, for the Tornado has unusually modest runway requirements for such a potent aircraft. In the filtered environment of the Personnel Briefing Facility, crews will plan their missions using the latest computerised equipment in order to match the accuracy of their aircraft's internal systems.

Having been given his target, the navigator will plot his route at the Cassette Preparation Ground Station (CPGS). Comprising a computer screen and keyboard linked to a magnetic map table, the CPGS records the aircraft flight-plan on a tape cassette almost identical to the type in widespread civilian use. To prepare his tape, the navigator places a map of the required scale on the table and enters two datum positions by pressing a button on the top of a cross-hair cursor which he slides over the surface. From this, the computer will deduce the map scale and north alignment. Next, the cursor is moved along the desired flight path, whilst the navigator enters letters beginning with 'A' to designate the position of each way-point (change of direction); numbers for each fix-point (a distinctive feature where the navigation can be cross-checked); and letters starting at 'X' for each target. As an added bonus the system will also compute fuel remaining at any point in the sortie. When inserted into the Tornado's central computer, the tape will fly the aircraft according to the pre-determined plan.

Automatic terrain-following capability is used by the Tornado to evade the defences by approaching at a height of 200ft (61m) in all weathers. When operating far into the rear areas, it will further improve its chances of success by making a stealthy approach to the target. Instead of bouncing radar waves off the intended victim for ranging purposes the navigator can select an 'initial point' (IP) up to 20 miles (32km) away, which may be to one side of the flight path. The IP should be a feature which shows clearly on the radar, and once this has been identified as a position check, radar can be switched off for a 'silent' run-in. Even if evasive action has forced the aircraft to approach from a different direction to that planned back at base, there is no problem as long as the radar can see the original IP. Weapon release is automatic, the computer taking into account the aircraft's speed and height, as well as the ballistic characteristics of the weapon to be dropped and the wind speed and direction.

The Tornado can fly a one-hour mission at the end of which its mean navigation system error is just 60ft (18m). Such accuracy cannot be matched by No 2 Squadron Jaguars, even with their new FIN 1064 nav/attack equipment, although use in the reconnaissance role still demands a high standard of navigation. Exploitation of the Jaguar's sorties is undertaken by the Reconnaissance Intelligence Centre (RIC) attached to No 2 Squadron in the form of a group of four mobile caravans and 10 trucks. (A similar unit is assigned to No 4 Squadron's Harriers and accompanies them into the field; No 2 is tasked to operate from Laarbruch, so its caravans are parked in a HAS on the airfield for protection.)

NATO specifications allow a maximum of just 45min between the Jaguar closing down its engines and the signalling back to TWOATAF HQ of a detailed report of findings. The six magazines, each holding 230ft (70m) of film, are first taken

Above:
Interpretation of a photo-recce sortie involves the pilot of a No 2 Squadron Jaguar GR1 in addition to an NCO (left) of the Reconnaissance Intelligence Centre. Five rolls of film (the forward-facing camera was not used on this mission), each 230ft long, are stretched over the light-table, and their spools may be advanced in unison. The sergeant interpreter is using a stereoscope on a negative strip from one of the oblique cameras.

Below:
NATO aircraft up to the size of a Transall C-160D have operated from strips of prepared autobahn during exercises, but none is more at home on such a surface than the Harrier.

Above:
Unusual 'customers' of a motorway service area on the A33 near Paderborn in September 1985 were Harrier GR3s of No 4 Squadron. Although regularly trained at field sites, the Harrier Force would probably operate from urban positions or motorways in wartime.

Below:
Since the West opted for unilateral chemical disarmament as a goodwill gesture, Soviet manufacture of such weaponry has increased manyfold. The only counter available to NATO is protection of personnel, pilots having the AR5 respirator. This is worn both on the ground and in the air to obviate the dangerous procedure of changing systems in the cockpit. A small compressor (here carried in the right hand) supplies air until the pilot can connect with the aircraft's oxygen supply, when it is left on the ground until landing. Pilots train with the AR5 at least once every six months.

by motorcycle to the RIC's processing caravan where they are normally developed, fixed, washed and dried by one machine at the phenomenal speed of 120ft (36.5m) per minute. If necessary this can be increased to 200ft (61m) by boosting the temperature of chemicals to 50°C. By using more than one machine, all six films can be completed in five minutes. There is no time for prints to be produced, so examination is made of the 70mm black and white film strips on a light-table, using a stereoscope to elicit detail. Some overlap exists between the fan of four F95 cameras which work in unison, the single forward-facing F95 and the vertically mounted linescan camera, and, if required, a wet print can be made in seconds to enhance the contrast of an unclear feature. (A steroscope cannot be used on linescan alone, because this produces a continuous picture rather than frames.) Whenever possible, the pilot will collaborate with the interpreter by adding his visual impressions of the sortie, although he is able to place a marker on the film margin during flight to draw attention to an important feature.

Operating in the defensive role, the two Wildenrath Phantom squadrons would be joined by a similarly-equipped unit of the USAF in wartime and assigned to interception of intruding aircraft. It is possible that they could be used to escort strike/attack missions, although the trend in recent years has been to provide the latter aircraft with enough self-defence equipment to fly without fighter cover. In order to keep combat readiness at a high pitch, pilots attend four training sessions per year in addition to the usual round of practices close to base with RAF and NATO aircraft. Training in air combat manoeuvring (ACM) takes place at Decimomannu, Sardinia, on a well-instrumented range and is undertaken in fortnightly deployments every six months. Missile camp at Valley, Anglesey, lasts two weeks per year, during which crews launch one Sidewinder or Sky Flash. Finally, with the gun still seen as an important weapon, four or five weeks annually are flown at Akrotiri, Cyprus, in conjunction with Canberra target tugs for pilots to gain the Allied Command Europe firing qualification.

Unlike their companions elsewhere in RAFG, Gütersloh's aircraft use concealment — not concrete — for protection in wartime. Field deployments are practised three times per year, the first being the appropriately-named Exercise 'Hard Frost' held in January or February and lasting a week. The spring exercise, 'Handy Forge', and that in autumn, 'Hazel Flute', last two weeks, the latter usually including a Taceval.

(Repetition of the letters 'HF' is explained by their also standing for 'Harrier Force'.)

In taking the field, the Harrier Force would deploy to six sites, plus a further location for the Forward Wing Operations Centre (FWOC) at which the Gütersloh station CO becomes the Harrier Force commander. Wartime sites would probably be in urban areas, but in the interests of public relations, training locations are in the countryside — sometimes on an army exercise area. The ideal urban site would be one offering a hard surface, such as a car park, with permanent buildings nearby, although the aircraft is quite capable of flying from a hastily-laid strip of aluminium planking. This would be laid by the army's Royal Engineers a day or two before the deployment, and comprises a take-off strip 425ft (130m) long and a landing pad 70ft (21m) square.

A Harrier site would be typically 10-60 miles (16-96km) behind the forward line of NATO troops, so giving a short flight time to the operational area, compared with that for the aircraft on permanent bases in the rear. In a five-hour period of sustained activity, a Harrier could fly 10 short sorties, whereas a Jaguar or Tornado unit in the far west of Germany would contribute only half that number during the same time. Around 200 sorties per day could be expected from the Harrier Force in the early stages of a conflict, falling off as attrition and servicing or battle damage repair requirements took their toll. Typically, the spares pack required by 10 aircraft operating off base for 14 days weighs about 7 tons (7.1 tonnes) and contains 650 items — one of which is an entire spare engine.

Defended from sabotage parties or lightly-armed enemy probes by the RAF Regiment, the Harriers would await their

Above:

A pilot's eye view of an exercise site for the Support Helicopter Force. Support trucks and tents are situated close to farm buildings, but in wartime would be placed in nearby trees and barns for concealment. Most civilians accept exercise disruption with good grace, and it is generally reckoned that pro-NATO sentiments increase in inverse proportion to the distance from the East German frontier.

Below:

The Chinook can carry up to 12 tons of supplies or 30 seated fully-equipped troops, although with seats removed the latter figure could be trebled in an urgent situation. The three hooks beneath the helicopter allow loads to be deposited at separate locations in seconds without landing. The centre hook is stressed to the full 12 tons, and the others to 9 tons each.

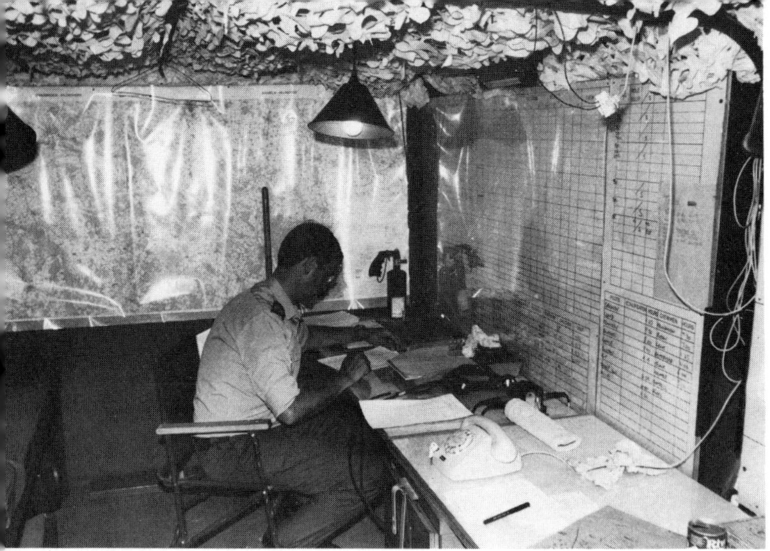

Above:
Located in the back of a truck, the helicopter Flight Control Centre is in contact with the Support Force HQ by radio and telephone. Tote boards on the right wall show six helicopters assigned to this Flight, whilst the map behind the duty sergeant is of the 1 (BR) Corps area.

Below:
Each year, Puma HC1 pilots of No 230 Squadron spend a long winter weekend at Bad Tolz, south of Munich, on the edge of the Bavarian Alps. Amid impressive scenery they practise flying in hazardous conditions, including landing on snow in a simulated troop-drop. Normal capacity is 16 fully-armed troops, or up to 5,500lb (2,495kg) of cargo.

instructions under the cover of camouflage netting beneath trees, or inside a barn or other hard structure. Close to each site is a fuel store sufficient for a day's flying, from which aircraft are replenished by bowser or from a pipeline laid to their hide. The rubberised 'fuel buns' in the store are refilled nightly from the larger, flexible 'pillow tanks' at the two field Logistics Parks attached to the Harrier Force. At the same time ordnance is delivered for the next day's missions.

The order for a sortie will originate in the Air Support Operations Centre (ASOC) which is located alongside the HQ of 1 (BR) Corps, and will often be as the result of a request for air support from an army unit in contact with the enemy. ASOC will then issue an Air Task Message to the FWOC, which allocates the task to a group or groups of Harriers via a VHF radio link. Each Harrier site has its Operations Officer, himself a pilot, and a Ground Liaison Officer from the army, working in collaboration with an intelligence officer. Army Air Force co-operation is vital at all stages of the tasking and flying process if disastrous misunderstandings are to be avoided.

Training for combat missions includes deployment to Decimomannu for three weeks per year, using the weapons range there for ground attack. The local Air Combat Manoeuvring range also sees the Harriers for a further fortnight. Every two years, three aircraft from each squadron fly to Cold Lake in Canada for a 'Maple Flag' training exercise with CAF and USAF allies. At such times there is opportunity to train with the nose-mounted Ferranti LRMTS, for in Germany only an eye-safe laser emitter on the ground can be used for training in target acquisition. Limited facilities are available for firing the Harrier's own laser on special ranges in Europe.

Helicopters too are spirited away from Gütersloh in time of conflict. Their deployment pattern is similar to the Harrier Force in that squadrons divide into three or more flights after receiving reinforcements from the OCU at home. Helicopters would perhaps take up residence in the corner of a field, close to woods, but farther forward than Harriers; Pumas closest to the front line, with Chinooks just behind. A typical Chinook site will comprise 60-70 personnel, four or five aircraft, an

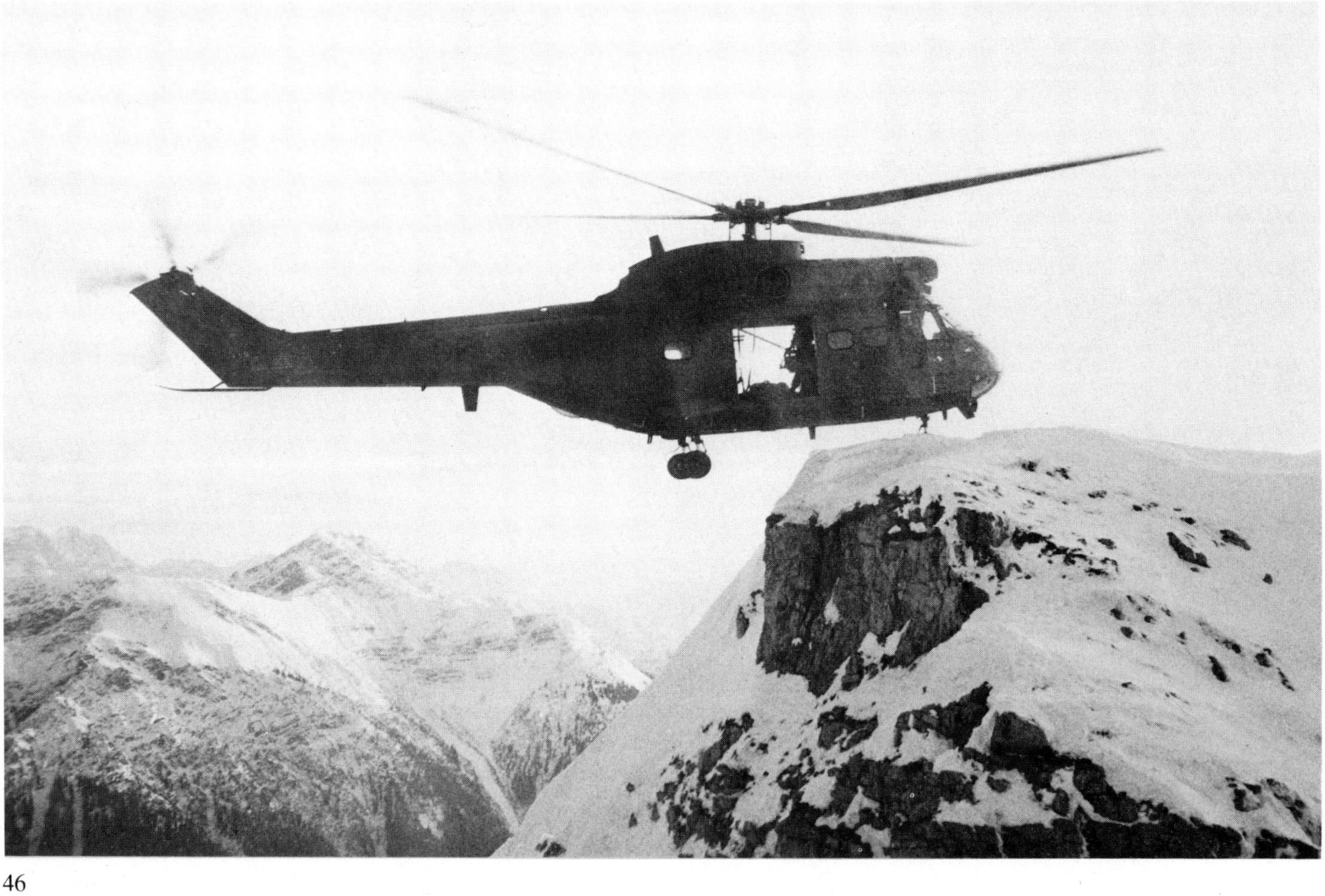

associated control centre (on the back of a lorry), plus maintenance equipment and tented living accommodation. Communications with the ASOC comprise UHF radio, the German telephone system (if working in wartime or TTW) and dispatch riders, enabling any site to assume the role of Helicopter Support Force HQ if necessary.

Fuelling of helicopters is at a Major Refuelling Area serving several sites, where stays are as brief as possible to minimise the risk of detection. It is not possible to manhandle Pumas and Chinooks across fields into woods to hide them at their sites, so they are parked as close as possible to trees or buildings and their Perspex covered with sacking to prevent glinting. Helicopters will be expected to operate in conditions of NBC contamination, so each flight has its own miniature refuge in the form of a Porton Liner. This is no more than a rubber tent and air-lock inflated by filtered air from a compressor so that inside pressure prevents the entry of impurities. Clearly not blast-proof, it does at least provide a rest-space where personnel can snatch a few moments of relaxation without having to wear a respirator and uncomfortable protective clothing.

Flying a large helicopter like the Chinook in a battle zone is an exacting task. Operating at altitudes so low that power cables are a hazard, the aircraft and those aboard can only rely on expert handling to save them if confronted by the enemy. Installation of radar warning receivers and associated protection is progressing steadily, and night vision goggles immensely expand the operating envelope, yet helicopter flying is almost as fatiguing as piloting a high performance jet. Chinooks are crewed by two officers plus an NCO loadmaster, and since 1985 one of the former two pilots has been replaced by a specialist navigator.

Although denied speed and silence with which to elude the opposition, the Chinook is not entirely devoid of guile. When several helicopters are tasked to deliver an army unit (perhaps

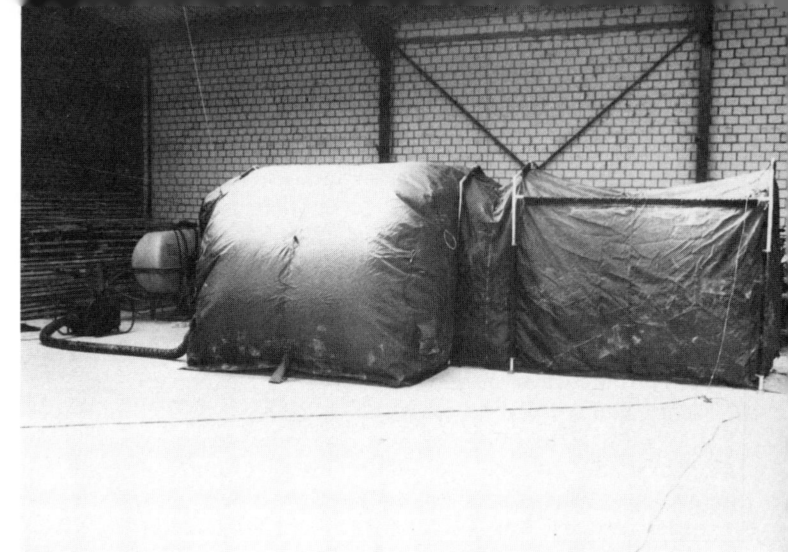

Above:
Providing a limited refuge from outside air contaminated with chemicals or fallout, the Porton Liner is a plastic tent and air lock (right) maintained at slightly higher than atmospheric pressure by a compressor (left, ground). Erected in a farm building on this occasion, this facility allows personnel to remove their uncomfortable NBC suits and respirators during brief rest periods.

Below:
Aircrew are trained in the art of self-preservation at the Winter Survival School, Bad Kohlgrub, near Oberammergau, Bavaria. Two-week courses of 35 students each are held every two weeks between January and March, their training including construction of shelters as well as trapping and evasion of 'enemy' search parties.

a rapid intervention force) to a dropping zone, they will approach from all points of the compass so low that they are out of sight to anyone who is not directly underneath the flight-path. The enemy on the ground will hear helicopters just as if they were in formation, but will be unable to give their true direction, thereby preserving some element of surprise for the airlifted troops. Such missions are practised with the army's 6 Brigade for maintaining rear area security and would be equally effective closer to the front line.

Keeping the helicopters and all RAFG's other assets up to peak efficiency is the command's principal peacetime task. At station level, 'Minival' exercises are held several times per year for some two days each, during which the base closes up to a wartime footing and practises security measures and aircraft mission launches. One or two times yearly this will be complemented by a 'Maxival' in which outside units are detailed to exercise the station. Typically, there would be air attacks and attempts to infiltrate the ground defences for sabotage. This culminates in the 'Taceval' (Tactical Evaluation) conducted at NATO level by the commander of Allied Forces Central Europe about once per year for each aerodrome.

There is a six-nation Taceval staff based at Ramstein for both TWO and FOURATAFs, comprising a small planning cell and between 100 and 120 examiners who are taken from their other duties as required. Tacevals are arranged in two parts, the first of which is a non-notice order to bring 70% of aircraft to readiness in under 12 hours. Points are awarded for performance, the units of RAFG normally achieving the required status in a fraction of the maximum time allowed. Some days later, part two of the Taceval will follow, including air attacks for which only three minutes' notice is given. Examiners test every aspect of the base, including security, battle damage repair to aircraft and installations, and medical care. Realism is assured by the notional introduction of bomb damage, chemical attacks, infiltrators and realistic-looking casualties.

Taceval ratings in all areas of performance are combined to give each station a grade which reflects its preparedness for war and can be directly compared with the marks achieved by other air forces. Any criticisms are made freely available to the base commander so that he knows in which aspects performance must be improved. Taceval results are classified secret on the grounds of security, yet a visitor to RAFG very quickly forms the impression that every station in the Command achieves the highest possible mark year after year. Excellent standards of training in a professional volunteer force and a first-rate esprit de corps are important contributory factors, as is the fact that self-contained units living on foreign soil usually have a faster reaction time than local troops, whatever the nationalities involved.

No matter by which method RAFG achieves its enviable Taceval record, the fact remains that throughout NATO it is known that Britain's dedication to European security is unquestionable. Although some members of the public at home still have difficulty in accepting Britain as a member of Europe, nobody on either side of the Channel can dispute the commitment which RAFG and BAOR symbolise. There may be sound financial reasons why it would be better to withdraw all RAFG aircraft to UK bases and replace them with a piece of paper promising their immediate return in time of need — as has already been done with some of their vital wartime supporting units. This would represent an unmitigated disaster for NATO and Europe, and the start of the fragmentation process which has long been sought by the Soviet Union and its Western fellow-travellers. Deterrence as practised by NATO depends upon providing a potential adversary with unambiguous, tangible evidence of cohesion and the willingness to react to aggression with single-minded determination. For as long as RAF Germany exists, Britain will be an inseparable component of Europe, and NATO will retain the credibility which preserves the peace.

Above:
Pumas extend their winter flying experience by assisting in the movement of survival trainees between camps during their fortnight at Bad Kohlgrub. At the same time, mutual experience is gained in SAR routines, including winching survivors out of confined areas.

Below:
Guard dogs are a valuable aid to security at all bases, the largest section being at Brüggen, where 46 are kept. Mostly Alsatians, all are donated by the public. A few of the 150 dogs in RAFG are trained as 'sniffers' for explosives and drugs, but their main duty is patrolling the miles of barbed wire surrounding aerodromes.